OTHER BOOKS BY F. N. MONJO

Indian Summer
The Drinking Gourd
The One Bad Thing About Father
Pirates in Panama
The Jezebel Wolf
Slater's Mill
The Vicksburg Veteran
The Secret of the Sachem's Tree
Rudi and the Distelfink
Poor Richard in France
Me and Willie and Pa
Grand Papa and Ellen Aroon
King George's Head Was Made of Lead
The Sea Beggar's Son
Letters to Horseface

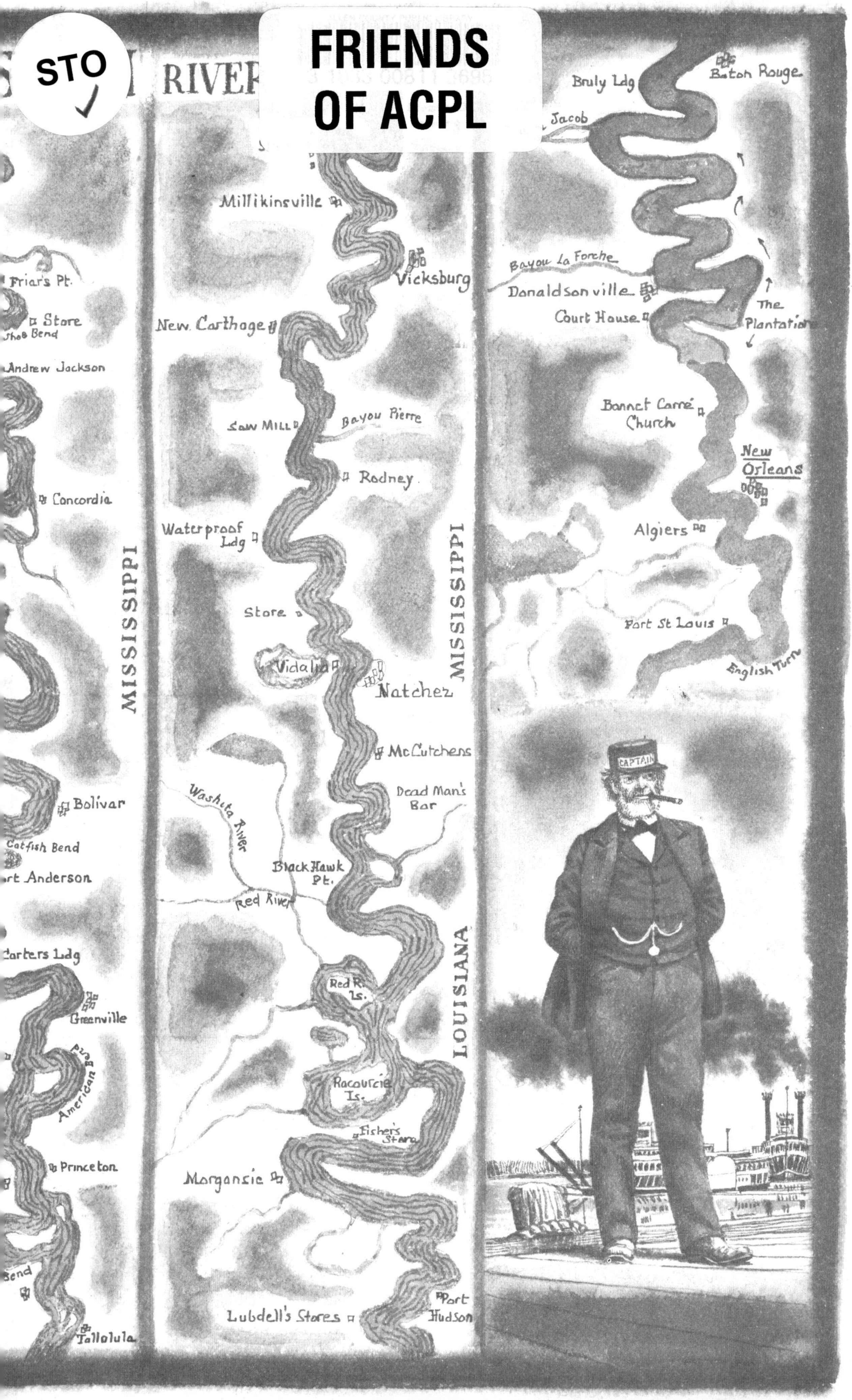
RIVER
Friar's Pt.
Store
Shoe Bend
Andrew Jackson
Concordia
MISSISSIPPI
Bolivar
Catfish Bend
rt Anderson
Carters Ldg
Greenville
American
Princeton
Bend
Tallolula
Millikinsville
Vicksburg
New Carthage
Saw Mill
Bayou Pierre
Rodney
Waterproof Ldg
Store
Vidalia
Natchez
MISSISSIPPI
McCutchens
Dead Man's Bar
Washita River
Black Hawk Pt.
Red River
Red R. Is.
LOUISIANA
Racourcie Is.
Fisher's Store
Morgansie
Lubdell's Stores
Port Hudson
Bruly Ldg
Baton Rouge
Jacob
Bayou La Forche
Donaldsonville
Court House
The Plantation
Bonnet Carré Church
New Orleans
Algiers
Fort St Louis
English Turn
CAPTAIN

WILLIE JASPER'S GOLDEN EAGLE

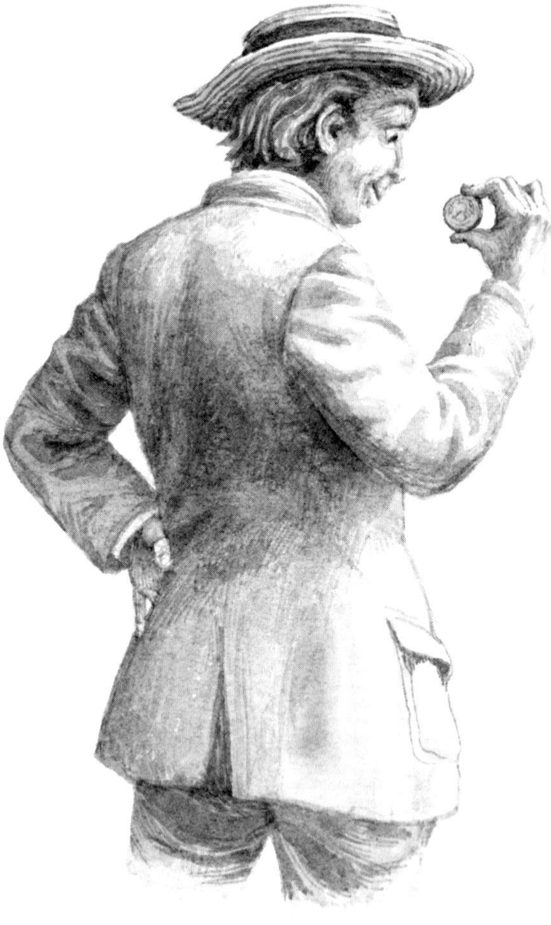

WILLIE JASPER'S GOLDEN EAGLE

*Being an Eyewitness Account
of the Great Steamboat Race
between the* Natchez *and the* Robert E. Lee

by F. N. MONJO

Illustrated by Douglas Gorsline

Doubleday & Company, Inc., Garden City, New York

Grateful acknowledgment is made to the following for permission to use copyrighted material:

LUDLOW MUSIC, INC.: For a verse from "The Good Old Rebel" (p. 24) Collected, Adapted and Arranged by John A. Lomax and Alan Lomax TRO - © Copyright 1934 and renewed 1962 LUDLOW MUSIC, INC., New York, N.Y. Used by permission.

HOLT, RINEHART AND WINSTON: For "On the Levee By the Riverside" (p. 48) from *Lower Mississippi* by Hodding Carter. Copyright 1942, © 1970 by Hodding Carter. Reprinted by permission of Holt, Rinehart and Winston.

Library of Congress Cataloging in Publication Data
Monjo, F N
Willie Jasper's golden eagle.
SUMMARY: An account of the famous 1870 steamboat
race down the Mississippi between the Natchez and the
Robert E. Lee, as told by a boy on board the Natchez.
[1. Steamboats—Fiction. 2. River life—Fiction.
3. Mississippi River—Fiction] I. Gorsline, Douglas W.,
1913– II. Title.
PZ7.M75Wi [Fic]
ISBN 0-385-02768-6 Trade
ISBN 0-385-02769-4 Prebound
Library of Congress Catalog Card Number 75-28455

Text Copyright © 1976 by F. N. Monjo
Illustrations Copyright © 1976 by Douglas Gorsline
All Rights Reserved
Printed in the United States of America
First Edition

*Dedicated to the memory
of men such as Leathers and Bixby,
who made of river life something akin to romance;
and especially to Mark Twain,
who commemorated it all so perfectly
in* Life on the Mississippi

Mark Twain in 1873

CONTENTS

Chapter One	*How I Got to Go to New Orleans*	11
Two	*On Board the* Creole Belle	14
Three	*Traveling Downstream*	21
Four	*In Natchez*	40
Five	*Down "The Coast"*	48
Six	*My Big Mistake*	59
Seven	*The Start of the Great Steamboat Race*	67
Eight	*What Happened at Natchez*	75
Nine	*Worse and Worse*	80
Ten	*The Bitter End*	87

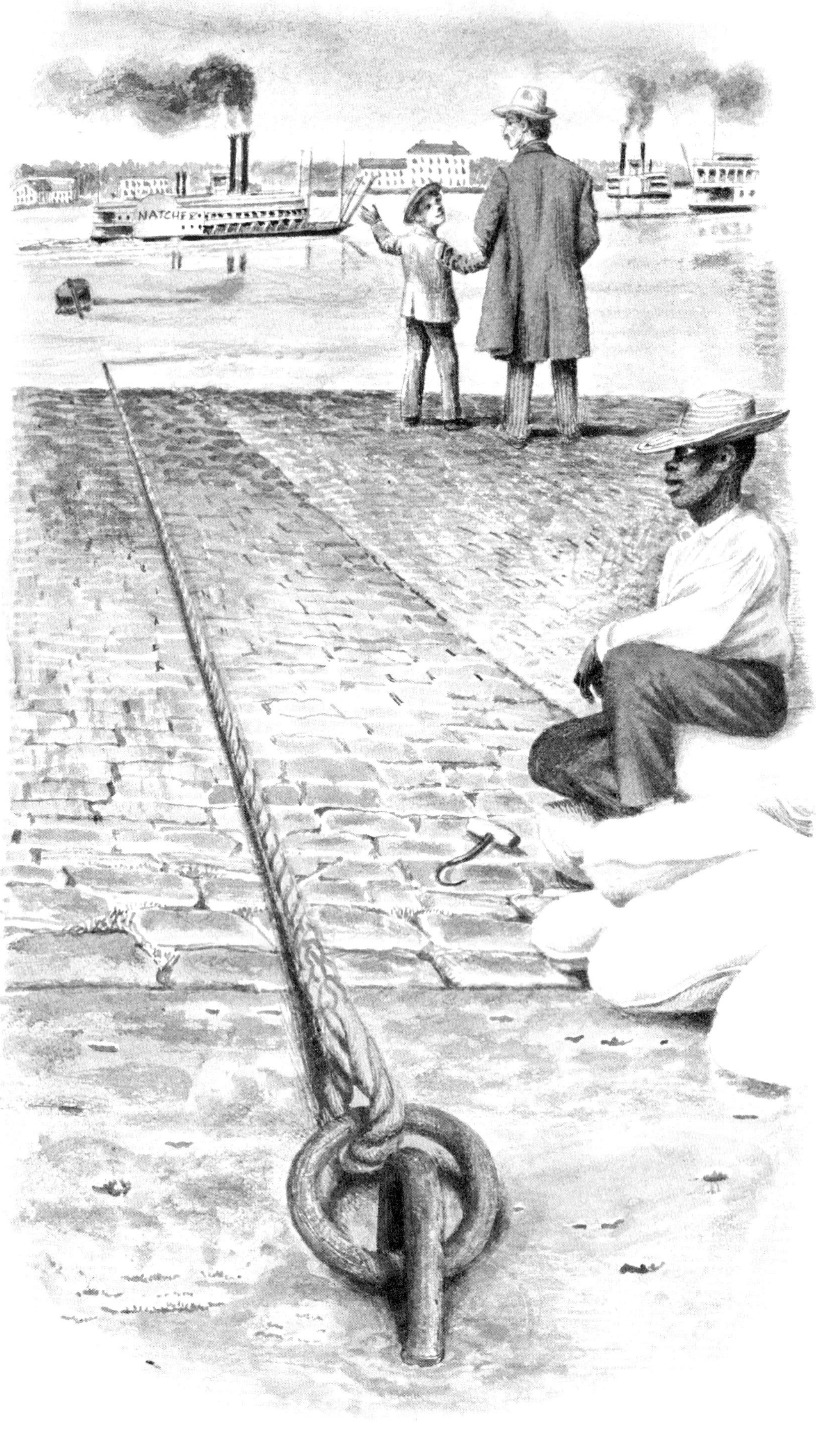

How I Got to Go to New Orleans

Mighty funny the way things turn out, sometimes. I never would have got to come along on that trip with Pa, if I hadn't been able to spell so good.

That's right. Toward the end of April, along when school was fixing to close, my fifth-grade teacher, Miss Rossiter, called Mamma in and told her that it looked like I was going to be failing my spelling and maybe my history, too. If I failed both of them, Miss Rossiter said, she didn't see how she could let me go on into sixth grade.

Mamma was just as angry as she could be when she heard that.

"You look here, Willie Jasper!" she said, giving me a good shake. "I don't aim to see you kept back like a dummy, you hear me? Any fool can learn to spell. And you're no fool. *No* child of mine is a fool. It's just you don't *apply* yourself."

Willie Jasper's Golden Eagle

And then she gave me a licking. And when Pa came home from his shoe factory that night and heard what had happened, he gave me another licking. That's the one I really remembered.

Well, Mamma and Pa commenced to hear my spelling. All kinds of four- and five-syllable words out of the blue-backed speller we use at school. Words like "alleviate," and "expectorate," and "indomitable," and "impenetrable"—words nobody *ever* uses. I was so scared I was going to be kept back, I studied hard and learned every one of them.

I just squeaked by on my history exam. But I won the spelling bee, when I turned out to be the only one in the whole school could spell "eleemosynary." Now that's a fool word most people can't even say, let alone spell. But I got it right. And Mamma was so happy she cried. And Pa was so pleased he give me a whole lot of money—a ten-dollar gold piece. An eagle! Twice as much money as I ever had at one time before.

I thought my good luck had quieted down for a spell, after that, what with me getting into the sixth grade, and all that money in my pocket. But I had another nice surprise coming.

You see, Pa had been planning to take Mamma with him on a business trip to New Orleans. But, instead, she got in "the family way," as they say, and of course I knew it. (Pa and Mamma didn't think I did.) I mean, after all, hadn't I seen Mamma get big, that way, when my brother Jay come along? And my next little brother, Reuben, too?

Of course, with the baby coming sometime in July, Mamma didn't want to go anywhere far from home. We live in Alton, Illinois, and my grandmother Parker lives there, too.

"I'll just stay here, with Mother and the children," Mamma told Pa, "and you go on without me."

Pa saw it wasn't no use to argue. Mamma was right. And even if she'd been wrong, she'd probably have gone on and done just what she made up her mind she was going to do.

"I wish I didn't have to go, either," said Pa. But we knew he had to, because he had his shoe factory to run, and if he didn't go down to New Orleans, how could he ever manage to buy the cotton he needed for shoe linings and such? At any price that he could afford, I mean.

"Maybe, since you can't come, Margaret," said Pa, "I'll see if old Eleemosynary, here, would like to be included."

I couldn't believe my ears! But as it turned out, he *meant* it. And by the eighth of June, we were in St. Louis, waiting to get on board the *Creole Belle,* and head downriver for New Orleans.

On Board the Creole Belle

St. Louis is some big city.

"Third largest in the United States," said Pa. We were standing in front of the Planter's House, early in the morning, waiting for the dray to come take our trunks down to the steamboat.

Once our two trunks were lifted in place and the driver and his mules had started off for the wharf, Pa decided we could just as well walk down to the embankment. We had plenty of time before the *Creole Belle* departed.

"I don't believe in gambling. And I don't believe in wasting money any other kind of way, either," said Pa.

"No, sir," I answered, feeling in my pocket to see if my golden eagle was still safe. It was.

I don't think I can tell you how busy that waterfront is, in St. Louis. Just thousands of steamboats come and go from this city, all year long. They have names like *Comet* and *Prairie* and *City of Pittsburgh,* and *Great Republic* and

On Board the Creole Belle

Grand Turk and *Fashion* and *Magnolia* and *Doubloon* and *Hiawatha* and *General Quitman*. And most times you see them curving away in a huge crescent, tied up half a mile or so, nosed in toward the river bank, just as thick as sucking pigs lined up against the belly of a sow. Pa told me there's not near as many boats on the river now, as there was before the rebellion. Then Pa laughed, and he said, "When we get down South, we'll have to start calling it 'The War Between the States.'"

I figured it was still the same Civil War, and that those Rebels had lost it, so I didn't care what I had to call it, just so long as I knew we'd won.

Anyway, before the war, ten years ago, Pa told me you could see a whole mile of river packets stretching up and down from the wharfboat on Walnut Street. They used to be lined up two and three deep in the river. Smoke from all their stacks made a billowing black cloud hanging over the city.

"Taking a trip on one of these steamers was something I dreamed about, but never could do, when I was a boy," said Pa.

Pa grew up on a farm, and he was real poor back then. He still loves steamboats just as much as he did when he was a boy. So I wouldn't tell him, for anything, that these fat, paddling river packets are too *slow* for me! It might break his heart if he thought he'd gone and had a boy didn't love them as much as *he* does.

They're graceful and pretty, I know. But do you realize they can't hardly move? Best they can do, coming upstream against the current, is about fourteen miles an hour! And it's 1,218 miles from St. Louis to New Orleans. So you figure out how long it's going to take us to get down there and back! Six or seven days just getting South, I make it.

Willie Jasper's Golden Eagle

'Course, going downstream, you don't have to fight the current, so you should make better time. But the fact is, when the river's low (like it is now, since the April floods are past) you're in much more danger of going aground on sandbars, or tearing your bottom out on snags and sawyers, so the captain generally ties up every night, and only dares run his boat by day, when his pilots can see the channel.

That's not what I call speed. When you're talking about *speed* give me the railroad. Big locomotive, booming and charging along, belching sparks and smoke, tearing up the track at thirty miles an hour. Maybe even forty, some day. Don't have to wait for anything. Going that fast you could go round trip to New Orleans and back quicker than we can go one way on the *Creole Belle*.

Right here in St. Louis you can see what's coming in the future. Just north of the city, on Bloody Island, there. You can see those big stone piers going up. Piers for that big

On Board the Creole Belle

railroad bridge across the Mississippi. They say it's going to cost *six million* dollars. Pa says Captain James B. Eads is building it. He's a river captain and a shipbuilder and a construction engineer, all rolled into one. I can't decide whether I'd rather be a locomotive engineer or a bridge builder, like Captain Eads. All I know is, I can't wait to see those big locomotives puffing over that bridge, once Captain Eads is done with it. They'll set some speed records, then, you can bet. Records that'll make the *Creole Belle* and all the rest of these steam packets look sick.

Don't get me wrong about this trip, now. I'm glad Pa asked me to come along with him. I knew I was going to enjoy every minute of it, and I did. I'd never been anywhere much outside of Alton, Illinois, before, except one trip to Springfield. I'd never been to Cairo, or Memphis, or Greenville, or Vicksburg, or Natchez, or Baton Rouge, or New Orleans—anyplace down South. I'd never seen any of them cities, so I was excited.

It's just that when folks talk about *speed,* I have to smile. You don't find speed on the river, these days. If you want speed, you ride the railroad. Any boy in Alton can tell you that much.

I mean, I'm talking about *today.* This is 1870. And these are go-ahead times. U. S. Grant is our President, and we Americans aim to show the world!

Pa keeps telling me that Grant is making some terrible mistakes, as President. But Pa fought for the Union in the war, and he loves Grant, because Grant won the war. And so I guess I love Grant, too. Pa's a pretty good man about most things, like President Grant and the Union. It's just he don't understand about speed and river packets and locomotives, like I do.

He tells me lots of things, though, and he's real kind and

Willie Jasper's Golden Eagle

good to me. I'm just ten, now, so I don't let on to Pa every time when I know he's wrong (which ain't that often).

"Soon's we get into our stateroom," said Pa, "I'm going to introduce you to Cap'n Henry Clay Dix, and ask him to show us over the boat. You reckon you'd like that?"

"Yes, sir," I said. And I meant it, too. The *Creole Belle* wasn't anywhere near the fastest boat on the river, and she sure wasn't anything like a locomotive, but she ran on *steam*. And I sure did want to have a chance to get a look at her boilers and engines and pistons and paddle wheels.

Pa told me it cost about fifty dollars to come upriver on a boat from New Orleans to St. Louis. But it only cost but twenty-five dollars to go down. Half-pints like me didn't cost but half of that.

Captain Henry Clay Dix turned out to be real jolly and nice. He had a fringe of white beard around his jaw, and snapping black eyes. He was old, but you could see he was smart. He'd been in this business nearly forty years—"with a three-year hiatus during the late unpleasantness," he said, with a laugh, and Pa laughed, too.

Now, "hiatus" ain't in my blue-backed speller, so far, so I wasn't sure what he meant by that expression. But I figured he meant that he couldn't run the *Creole Belle* while they was fighting the war. He's lucky she didn't get sunk by gunboats, Pa said, like so many of them did.

The boat was just beautiful. I mean, she may not have been a locomotive, but she was pretty! She had these two great big paddle wheels, each one about as tall as a three-story building. And she had three decks, and these great big driving rods turning her paddle wheels, and two huge, black smokestacks, and a steering wheel up in the pilothouse reaching up two feet over Captain Dix's head—and that was only *half* of it, because the other half was set down into the texas—into the deck below! I sure wish Captain Dix had asked me to take hold of that wheel for ten or fifteen minutes. Just holding onto that thing would have made me feel as if I was just about two feet taller than Pa!

Sometime around 8:00 in the morning, just after Pa and I came aboard, the pilot came up into the pilothouse. Captain Dix turned over the navigation of the ship to him.

There was a whole lot of tooting, and some bells commenced jingling down below, and Mr. Samuels, the pilot, hollered into the speaking tube that goes down into the engine room:

"Back her, Ned, half speed."

And the ropes holding her to the wharf were thrown off, and the *Creole Belle* backed out into the river.

Couple of other steamboats tooted when they saw we was leaving.

We turned tail on St. Louis and headed south down the river, toward Cahokia and Carondelet.

Of course, the Missouri pours into the Mississippi a few miles *above* St. Louis, as everyone knows. And they don't call the Missouri "the Big Muddy" for nothing. All I'm trying to say is, once that load of mud from the Missouri slides into the Mississippi, that old river looks like coffee-with-cream, from there on down.

At Alton, where I live, the Mississippi is fairly clear. But after the Missouri comes pouring in from the west, it's a different story.

"It looks just like mud," said Pa, "from here on down to New Orleans."

Many times as I've seen it, it's still surprising how big and wide the river is. You can *see* how powerful she is, just watching her roll along. Rolling and boiling and twisting, in big, oily heaves, like a huge brown sea monster. And mysterious ripples on the surface that look like they might be bubbling up from the center of the earth.

It turned out that Captain Henry Clay Dix, and Mr. Samuels, the pilot, never did let old Willie Jasper get his hands on that wheel up in the pilothouse. Mostly because the river was so low, just then, I reckon. But I knew I'd get to learn something about steamships and steam engines, just the same.

Traveling Downstream

Captain Henry Clay Dix asked Pa and me to come up and visit with him in the pilothouse after we got our stuff stowed in our stateroom.

I got kind of hot and sleepy up there, that morning, watching the sun sparkling and dancing on the water. The *Creole Belle* stayed out in midstream, carried along by the swift current. The pounding of her big engines and the churning of her paddles helped make me sleepy, too. It got hazy and muggy as the morning wore on. Both banks were kind of gray-green and foggy. Nobody along the bank signaled for us to land, so we swept right on past Jefferson Barracks and Oakville and Finestown.

"I expect we'll stop at St. Genevieve sometime after midday dinner," said Captain Dix. Then he set his black eyes on me. "You know something, boy?" said Captain Dix. "Mr. Samuels might have cut into that chute behind that island, right there, and saved us a mile or two, if there was more water in the channel than we got today."

"Might have tried it today," said Mr. Samuels, "if we'd

Willie Jasper's Golden Eagle

been coming upriver, *against* the current. But going down, this way, with the current sweeping us along from behind, I can't be sure I can hold this old mud turtle in her marks, along the channel."

I nodded my head and stood as close to the wheel as I dared. I wished Mr. Samuels had let me take her just for a second. But he didn't.

Captain Dix called into the speaking tube to order three black coffees.

"I reckon Willie Jasper'll take some sarsaparilla," he said, giving me a wink.

"Yes, sir," I said. So he hollered that down the tube, too, telling them to put in plenty of ice.

By the time the waiter came up in his white jacket, with the coffees and the icy mug of sarsaparilla, the men had started talking about the war, and speed records on the river, and things of that kind. From the drift of their talk, I figured Mr. Samuels and Captain Dix must have fought for the Union, against the South, same as Pa had.

"You hear about Tom Leathers?" said Captain Dix to Pa.

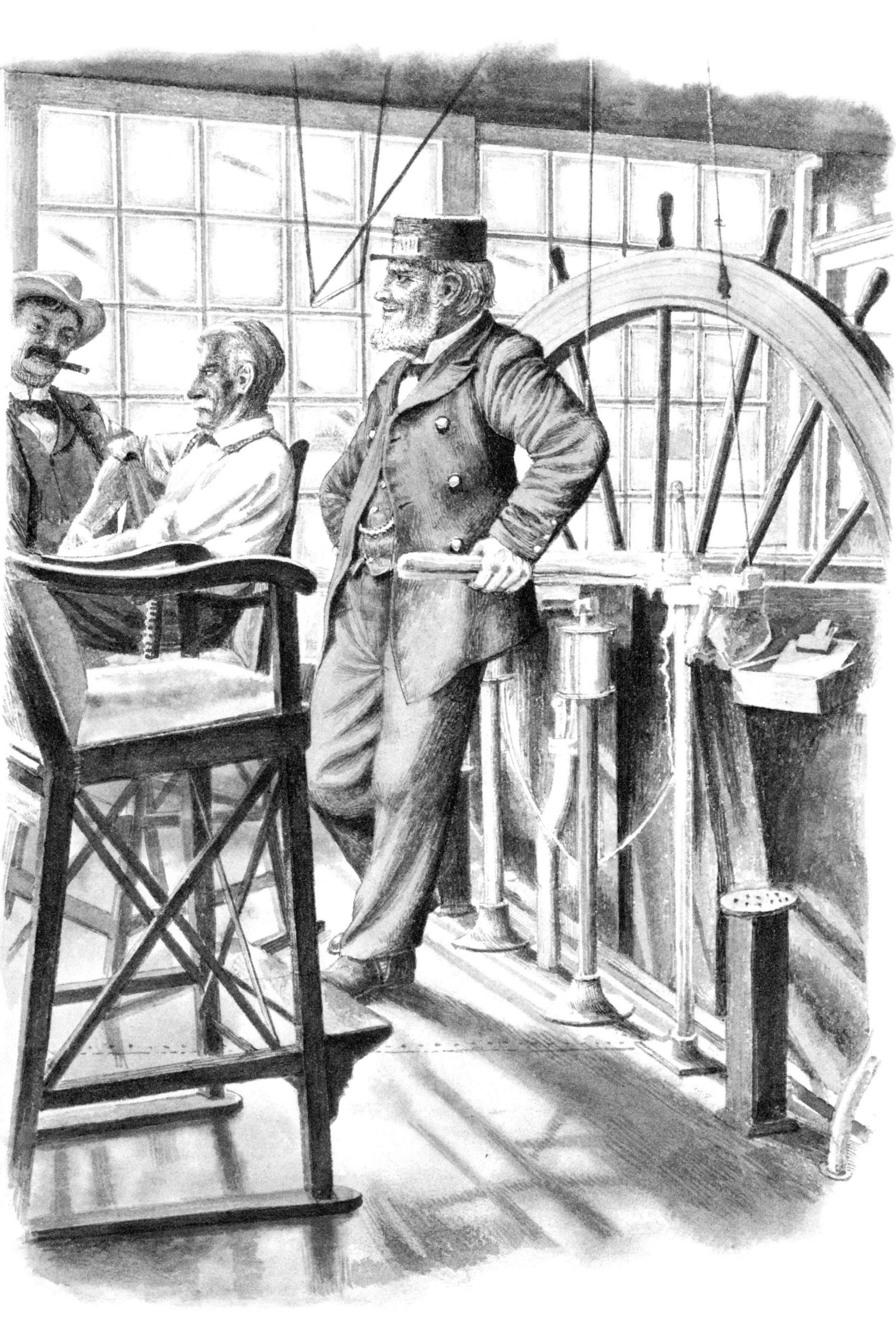

Willie Jasper's Golden Eagle

"Big, red-bearded fellow from Kentucky?" said Pa.

"That's him," said Mr. Samuels. "He's captain of the *Natchez*."

"One of the best captains on the river," said Captain Dix, "even if he is the most unreconstructed rebel you're ever likely to meet."

"Unrecon*structed!*" said Mr. Samuels, with a whoop. "Why, that old scoundrel Leathers won't even fly the American flag on his boat, to this day, even though the war is long since over, and Lincoln in his grave for more than five long years."

And with that, he began chuckling and singing:

> Oh, I'm a good old rebel,
> Now that's just what I am;
> For this "fair land of freedom"
> I do not care a damn.
> I'm glad I fit against it,
> I only wish we'd won.
> And I don't want no pardon
> For anything I've done . . .

"Yes, indeed," laughed Captain Dix. "That's Captain Thomas P. Leathers to a T—master of the steam packet *Natchez,* sixth boat to bear that glorious name. His fifth *Natchez,* I suppose you know, he turned over to the rebel navy. They tried to fit her up for a ram, and covered her with cotton bales, for protection, but Captain Eads burned her to the water's edge, 'way down in the delta bayous, back in '63. And Leathers has been sore at all the rest of us, ever since."

The men laughed, and began talking for a while about southern politics. Things I didn't understand. About the Freedmen's Bureau, and the Ku Klux Klan, and carpetbaggers and scalawags.

I wanted to ask a world of questions about what they was

Carpetbaggers and scalawags

Willie Jasper's Golden Eagle

saying, but you can't usually get a word in edgewise when grownups are talking amongst themselves. And if you butt in, they generally don't answer you anyway.

"Yes, Lord," said Mr. Samuels, easing off the wheel of the *Creole Belle* just a spoke or two, as she began making her way around a piney cape of land. He spat a stream of tobacco juice into a shiny brass cuspidor, two yards from where he stood. "We hear, Mr. Jasper," he said to Pa, "that Tom Leathers is fixing to try to break a record, this month, on the New Orleans–St. Louis run."

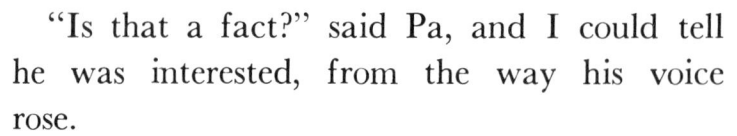

"Is that a fact?" said Pa, and I could tell he was interested, from the way his voice rose.

"Yes, sir," said Captain Dix, sipping the last of his coffee, "twenty-six years ago, back in eighteen and forty-four, the *J. M. White* made that run to St. Louis in three days, twenty-three hours, and nine minutes. And now, Tom Leathers thinks he can better it, with the *Natchez.*"

He and Pa began talking about boats and records. About the *A. L. Shotwell,* and the *Eclipse,* and about another boat Captain Leathers used to own, called the *Princess,* that still holds the horns for her 17½-hour run from New Orleans to Natchez—268 miles. I figured out that that's just a little better than 15 miles an hour, and I'm sorry, but I couldn't call that *fast,* so I just kept my mouth shut and let them talk away amongst themselves.

(Above and opposite) *Riverboat captains*

Traveling Downstream

"Mr. Samuels, sir," I said, "why do they talk about 'holding the horns'? What does that mean?"

He laughed and pointed down toward the hurricane deck. "You see that big bell, there, Willie?"

"Yes, sir."

"Well, if this old mud turtle wasn't so wheezy that she'd be sure to bust a boiler if I was to get up a real head of steam in her, you just might see some horns on *that* bell."

"Don't you *think* about trying to race my *Creole Belle*," said Captain Dix. "Her boilers couldn't stand it, and neither could I. I'm a low-pressure captain, and I want to stay that way. Caution and safety are my watchwords. I haven't steamed or broiled or barbecued a passenger to death, yet—like quite a few captains I could mention."

All the men laughed. Then Mr. Samuels turned to me again, and lowered his voice so Captain Dix couldn't hear.

"No, you wouldn't dare race this old mud turtle," he said, with a sigh. "But when a boat *does* make a record run on the river, from New Orleans to Louisville, or something like that, they present the winning captain with a set of gilt elk antlers, you see, and he fastens them up there, forward, on either side of the bell on the hurricane deck."

"And that's why they say he holds the horns?" said I.

"Yep," said Mr. Samuels. And he spat another stream of tobacco juice into the cuspidor. "Makes a world of difference, too, when a boat holds the horns. Everybody wants to ship their goods on a fast boat. And passengers want to brag that they been riding her, too. That means the steamboat company can put the rates up and charge more money for fares and freight."

Mr. Samuels pointed out a little town called Rush Tower on the Missouri shore, and told me that I better go down and wash up for dinner, because it was getting near time for a great big meal of fancy fried chicken and biscuits and rice and gravy, down in the main cabin, and it would be served up pretty quick, now.

Soon after this, Pa and I went down to our stateroom to get ourselves tidy for dinner. We had a double bed in our stateroom, and a good-sized window, opening out onto the boiler deck. And there was a big marble-topped washstand in there, with a large round bowl, and a pitcher, and some soap and towels. And when you rang for the chambermaid, she'd bring you plenty of hot water.

Pa and I wanted to look as genteel as possible, because Pa explained to me that meals on one of these big river packets are very special affairs. They are, too. Because everybody eats a lot, and they serve four, five, six, seven courses of food!

Pa and I don't eat all that much at home. But he told me on the steam packets, they *expect* you to eat as much as you can hold. It's all part of the fare.

They have big tables set up, running down the middle of the main cabin, under colored glass skylights in the ceiling. For centerpieces, they have big blocks of clear ice, with real roses and other flowers frozen right in, to look pretty. Captain Dix told us those flowers were frozen in, that way, down in Natchez at the ice plant they have there.

At every place at the table they set up the knife and fork

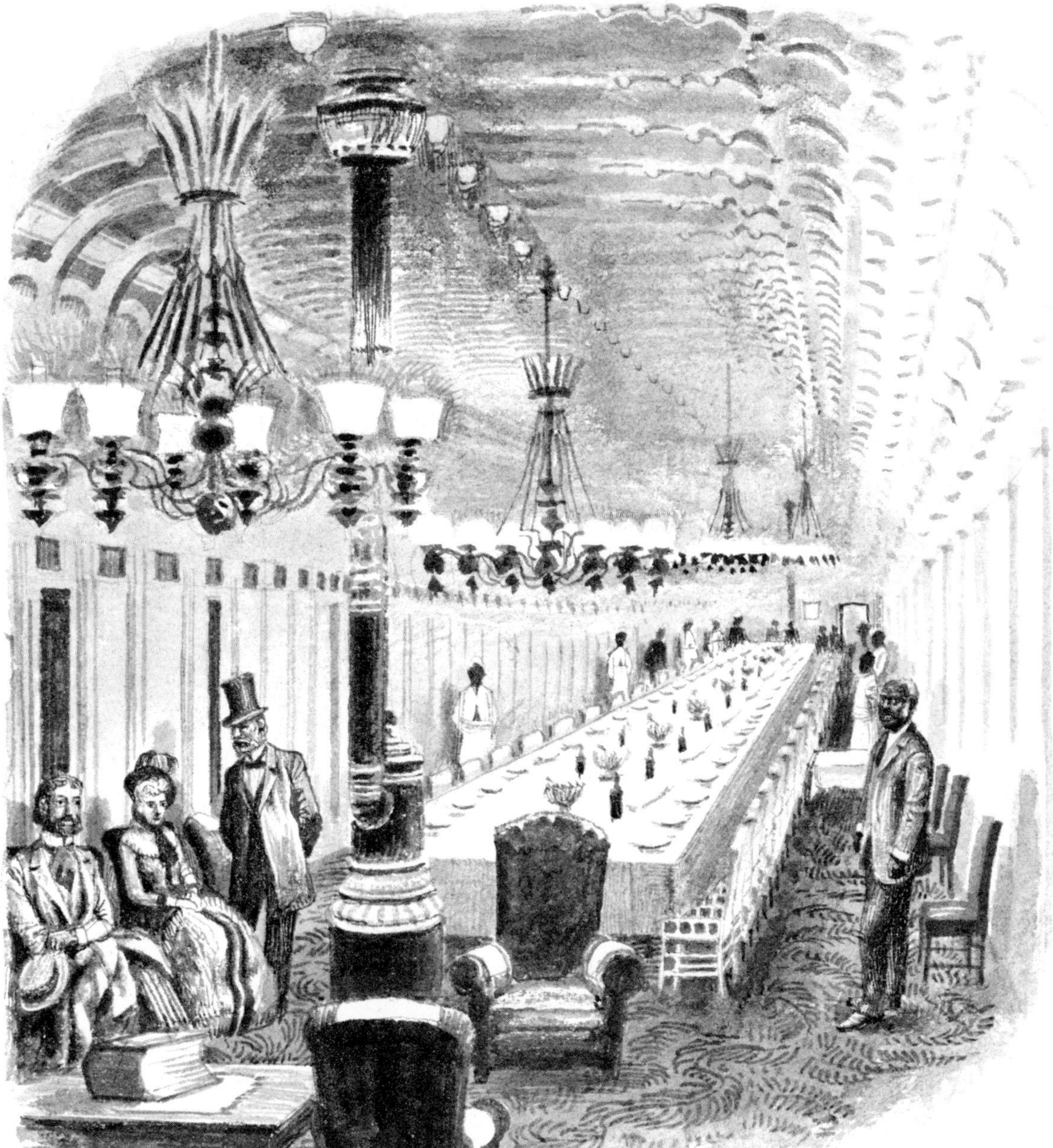

Riverboat gamblers

Traveling Downstream

and spoon in a little tripod, over the plate. I couldn't figure out how they ever got them to balance. And they twist up the napkins, like flowers, and set them in the empty water glasses, pretty as a picture. Waiters in white coats stand right behind you, ready to bring you anything you want.

There was a world of ladies in bustles and silk skirts and flounces, with shawls and parasols and little hats that sat kind of over one eye. And gentlemen with canes and flowered waistcoats and tight britches and plug hats.

They sure could eat!

Here's what Pa and I had: crayfish bisque—that's a thick soup made of river shrimp. And baked red snapper—that's a real good fish they stuff and bake. And baked prairie hen. And wild rice. And lemon sherbet. And roast beef. And fried chicken. And six kinds of dessert. I'm not joking! There was wine jelly, and custard, and chocolate cake, and cherry pie, and apple pie, and fresh fruit. It's a wonder I didn't get sick.

Pa said he didn't understand how the steam-packet companies could feed folks as good as they do. I don't understand it, either. I was stuffed!

When dinner was over, the ladies all went into their cabins for a nap, and I was sleepy, too.

Pa said, "Now, Willie, while we're on this boat, you watch out that you don't let some river gambler get hold of your eagle!"

That made me put my hand in my pocket to see if my ten-dollar gold piece was still there. It was just where it ought to be.

Pa told me that sometimes on these riverboats card-sharps start up gambling games in the men's cabin, where the bar is. Usually at night. Sometimes passengers will gamble and lose their farms and houses. Even their wives' jewelry! Before the war, they might gamble away whole plantations and all their slaves!

I guess that's why Pa said I should watch out for my eagle.

But after a big meal like that, who'd want to play cards? Besides, it turned out there wasn't any gamblers on the *Creole Belle,* anyway. I guess she must have been too slow-moving for them.

I was kind of drowsy that afternoon, after all that food. We passed the mouth of Establishment Creek, then we went by Prairie de Rocher, and around three we churned right up to the landing at St. Genevieve, docked, and put down our gangplank.

There was passengers getting on and off. And a lot of freight to be loaded. You should have seen those roustabouts heaving sacks of coal on board, for the ship's fires. They was rolling barrels up and down the gangplank, too, as if they was nothing. Those men are strong as they can be. Each one of them a black Hercules. Huge arms and deep chests. And they sing while they work:

> I hear that bell a-ringing
> I see the captain stand
> Boat done blowed her whistle
> I know she gwine to land.
> I hear the mate a-calling,
> "Go git out the plank,
> Rush out with the headline,
> And tie her to the bank."
>
> Roll out, heave dat cotton.
> Ain't got long to stay.

During the rest of that afternoon on the first day, we ran down past Kaskaskia and New Bourbon and Chester and Liberty. Then we passed St. Omer's Island, and Lagourse's Island. But when we got down far as Fountain Bluff, just

Traveling Downstream

above Grand Tower, Captain Dix decided he was going to pull into Breesville and tie up for the night.

"Bad stretch of river from here down to Cairo," he said. "We can't chance it any further than this, with evening coming on."

Around eight o'clock Pa and I went down to the main cabin for another big meal, same as we had had at dinner. All the big kerosene chandeliers with their frosted globes was blazing, and everything was shined and polished and fixed and served just so. After that, we went up onto the hurricane deck to sit for a while, and look at the river in the moonlight.

We saw a few boats pass us, going upriver, north to St. Louis. One was the *Great Republic,* and the other was the *Judge McClean.*

You could hear the leadsmen, two on either side of each of the ships, calling up to the captain and the pilot. First they'd throw out the lead line, then pull it in again measuring the depth of the channel. Then the starboard leadsman would sing out:

"Half twain."

Then the larboard leadsman would heave and call:

"Half tha-reeeee!"

Pa said the first cry meant that there was fifteen feet of water, and the second meant twenty-one feet.

Since these river packets didn't usually draw but eight or nine feet, they had nothing to worry about there.

Then, once they'd get up above the Devil's Bake Oven, we'd hear the leadsmen calling their ghostly call:

"Captain, I got no-o-o-o-o-o bottom."

And Pa said that meant the channel was over twenty-four feet deep. And after *that,* it was so deep they quit calling, and the ships chugged on up the river, into the night. I

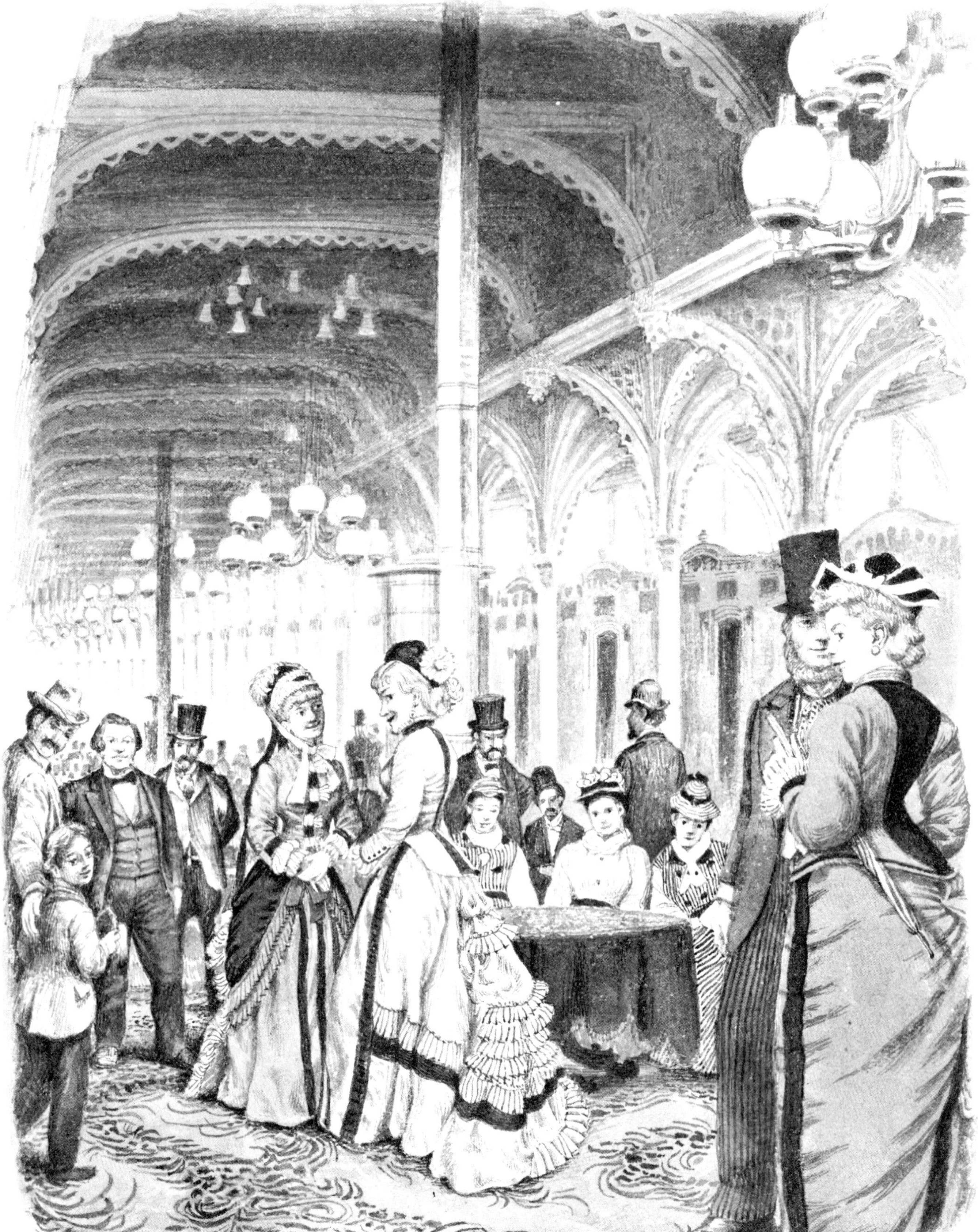

Traveling Downstream

watched their lights, and the sparks pouring out of their smokestacks. Then they'd disappear from sight, in the trees beyond the bend, and quiet and blackness would settle down over the river. Except for some frogs croaking. And some insects clicking. And the river gurgling by. And a few little lights glimmering on the water, from over Breesville way.

The days was pretty much like that all the way down to New Orleans. We didn't meet any gamblers, so there weren't any fistfights or any shootings on the ship. We didn't hit any snags, or sawyers, hidden in the river, so we didn't sink. And Captain Dix and Mr. Samuels never raced her, so our boilers never came anywhere near blowing up. We stayed quite safe, plowing along on our old mud turtle, the *Creole Belle*.

Some days we'd stop at a landing to pick up some mules and some barrels of molasses. Or we'd nose into a woodyard, and the roustabouts would load us up with fat pine or sacks of coal, whatever Captain Dix needed for his boiler fires in the engine room.

When we passed Thebes, Illinois, Captain Dix told me that the next three miles were one of the worst stretches of the river—from Thebes to Commerce—because there were a lot of sunken rocks at this point. Pilots called them "the Grand Chain," and he said a world of steamships had gone down here, wrecked and sunk and ruined. Plenty of people drowned, too.

Soon after, we rounded Dog Tooth Bend and got to Cairo, where the Ohio comes in. Pa told me that the old French settlers, who were the first white people out here in the valley, used to call the Ohio *la belle rivière*—the beautiful river—because it was so clear and pretty and green, back in those early days. It's not half so muddy as the Mississippi, even now.

"When the first Americans came out this way, son," said Captain Dix, "they must have thought they'd struck the river Nile! How else can you account for all those Egyptian names they gave these towns? Cairo? Thebes? Memphis?"

I didn't say much, because I hadn't guessed there was towns with such names in Egypt. But I expect Captain Dix must know what he's talking about—though why those fool pioneers thought they'd got to Egypt really beats me.

Below Cairo, they commence giving numbers to the islands in the river. Like Island No. 1 and Island No. 2. Island No. 6 is near Hickman, Kentucky. Island No. 10 is just above

New Madrid, Missouri. Pa says there was a big naval battle there, during "the late unpleasantness"—or the War Between the States, as I'd been told I'd better call it once I got down in Dixie.

It was real lazy, going down the river. It takes over an hour to pass Riddle's Point, just before you come to Mrs. Merriweather's Landing. Then on to Walker's Bend and Pilgrim's Island. Off in the distance you can see the little town of Osceola, Missouri, just opposite Plum Point, Tennessee.

Willie Jasper's Golden Eagle

One of the things that slows you down is oxbows. They're great big meandering curves in the river, shaped kind of like this:

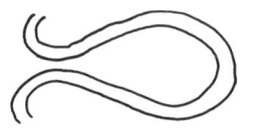

where the river curves way back on itself. Sometimes it's fourteen, fifteen miles around a bend like that. Captain Dix told me you could walk across the neck—about a mile or so wide—quicker'n the steamboat could make it by river, in some places!

I thought to myself: that's just another reason why the railroad's going to put these old mud turtles out of business. A locomotive can travel in a straight line on a track. But a steam packet has to double back on itself, and twist and turn, however the river winds.

Below Plum Point, you pass the first Chickasaw Bluff, and the mouth of the Hatchee River. Then you come to the second Chickasaw Bluff, and Pecan Point. The third Chickasaw Bluff and the Devil's Race Ground. Then Beef Island. And finally the city of Memphis, sitting high up, on the fourth Chickasaw Bluff.

Right above Memphis there's a cluster of five islands they call Paddy's Hen and Chickens. It was right about there, Pa told me, that the steam packet *Sultana* blew up. It was five years ago, and she was carrying thousands of soldiers back up north, right after the war. Pa said hundreds and hundreds of the poor fellows were scalded to death by steam. And plenty more drowned. A ghastly wreck!

We spent the night tied up at the levee in Memphis. So, that evening, Pa took me up to the Gayoso Hotel, and I sat in the lobby for a spell while he had a drink at the bar.

Traveling Downstream

The next day, we passed Helena, Arkansas, up on her bluffs. There the river commenced to get broader. Full of curves as a corkscrew, with huge cypress trees lining the banks, standing knee-deep in water.

When you get down into Mississippi and Arkansas, where we were by then, they quit calling the streams "creeks," mostly, and commence calling them "bayous." Pa said plenty of them bayous had alligators in 'em! And we began to see moss hanging from the trees.

I don't remember every place we were, but there was Catfish Point and Cypress Bend and Yellow Bend and Spanish Moss Bend and Steele's Bayou and Terrapin Neck.

Then we came to Milliken's Bend, and Pa told me that's where Grant's men waited while he tried to figure out how to capture Vicksburg, just down below. And then, on the high bluffs of the Walnut Hills, you see Vicksburg itself—the "Fortress of the Confederacy"—where the rebs had fourteen miles of cannon, until they had to surrender everything to Grant, on July 4, 1863.

We stopped there for a few hours, and Pa took me up into the town and bought me dinner at the Prentiss House.

On our way down below Vicksburg, in the afternoon, Pa showed me where President Grant (he was a *general*, of course, during the war) fought some battles. Places named Grand Gulf and Bruinsburg and Bayou Pierre and Rodney. Pa said there was a little town some ways up Bayou Pierre called Port Gibson—a town that Grant had said was "too pretty to burn."

Late that afternoon we got to the town of Natchez, sitting way up high on some bluffs two hundred feet above the river. And Captain Dix said he reckoned we'd tie up there for the night.

In Natchez

There's no high ground at all on the west bank of the Mississippi after you get down past Helena, Arkansas. All Louisiana is just as flat as a pancake. But there's plenty of hills on the *east* bank, on the Mississippi shore. And some of the prettiest and highest of those hills are at Natchez.

Captain Dix said we'd be staying tied up at the landing in Natchez until 7:30 the next morning, so Pa and I had plenty of time to explore the town.

Some of the ladies on the *Creole Belle* hired barouches, so they could drive over to Brown's Gardens, a half mile above the landing, to see the beautiful plantings of camellias and gardenias they have there.

Pa asked Captain Dix and Mr. Samuels to come up on top of the bluff to a big hotel there called the Mansion House and drink some of their famous mint juleps with him. They accepted.

Captain Dix told us that before the war, maybe twenty, thirty years ago, Natchez-under-the-Hill was full of grog

In Natchez

shops and gambling dens, and they used to have lots of knifings and shootings there. Most all of those old buildings have caved into the river by now, because the Mississippi keeps eating into the bank there.

Captain Dix said one time a mate on one of the packets tied up in Natchez was cheated out of a whole bunch of money in a crooked faro game at a gambling house that sat there under the hill, right on the river's edge.

When the mate told his captain how he'd been cheated, that tough old captain got his engines going, tied a great big hawser from his boat clear around the gambling house. Then he began backing his packet out into the river. He threatened to pull that rickety old building right smack into the water, unless somebody saw to it that the mate got his money returned to him in double-quick time.

"Those walls of the gambling house began creaking and shaking and groaning," said Captain Dix, "and you can bet that that mate got all of his money back in a hurry—right down to the last penny!"

Mr. Samuels showed me the set of gilded six-pronged elk antlers fixed high up on a post on board the Natchez wharfboat. They're the horns that Captain Tom Leathers won and placed there fourteen years ago, when he covered the 268 miles from New Orleans to Natchez in record-breaking time, in his beautiful new *Princess*.

"He made that run in 1856, in the time it says right there on that sign," said Mr. Samuels. "Broke the record fourteen years ago, and it still stands to this day."

I looked up at the elk antlers, and read the lettering on the sign:

Princess' time to Natchez
17 hours and 30 minutes.

There was a metal tag hung between the tips of the antlers. On this tag was painted:

WHY DON'T YOU TAKE THE HORNS?

"From what I hear about Captain Cannon, of the *Robert E. Lee,*" said Captain Dix, "he just may be fixing to try to take those horns, at that!"

Turned out that Pa and Captain Dix and Mr. Samuels didn't have such a good opinion of Captain Cannon. They said he'd raised the money to build his ship down around Shreveport, Louisiana, during the war. They said he bought up hundreds and hundreds of bales of contraband cotton that the rebels should have burned, but didn't. Then he got hold of it somehow and shipped it all up to St. Louis, where he got a great big price for it. Cotton got mighty scarce up North, it seems, during the war.

And another reason they didn't like Cannon much—he was a Yankee himself, same as they all were. But everybody was saying that he'd named his new ship the *Robert E. Lee* because he was fixing to go into the New Orleans to Vicksburg trade. And Cannon knew everybody down South just worshiped the name of Old Marse Robert E. Lee, the best general the Confederacy had. So by putting Lee's name on his ship, Cannon figured he'd be helping his *business!*

We climbed the steep, dusty road that leads up to Broadway, on top of the Natchez bluffs. There Captain Dix showed us a big, pink brick house, named Rosalie, where General Grant stayed for a few days, back in '63, when Natchez was occupied by the Union Army.

Then we crossed a wooden footbridge that spans a big gully there, on top of the bluff. From that bridge you get a wonderful view of the river.

We all four of us hired a carriage and drove around the

In Natchez

town for an hour or two, until sunset, seeing the sights. Pa said Natchez used to have a big race track called Pharsalia, before the war, and a big social season, whatever that is.

"Why they should have named the track for the place where Pompey lost his battle with Julius Caesar is more than I can tell you," said Pa.

Pa likes to brag some about knowing ancient history. I don't even know who Pompey was.

Captain Dix says there are fifty or sixty beautiful big houses still standing in the Natchez district—houses that didn't get burned up in "the late unpleasantness," because most of the fighting was up around Vicksburg, not down near Natchez.

"You see, the land is high, here," said Captain Dix, "and cooler than it is over there in hot, flat Louisiana. So, the wealthy planters who grew cotton or sugar cane, over there, would build themselves a big town house, over here in Natchez, where the air is better. Thought they might get away from the yellow fever that way, too. But it didn't do much good, because the fever struck here many times, same as everywhere else."

"I understand that plenty of those old rascals were so rich that they didn't favor secession, when the sovereign state of Mississippi began to think of taking leave of the Union," said Pa.

"Quite true," said Mr. Samuels. "Many of the planters here weren't Democrats. Weren't 'Bourbons,' or 'fire-eaters,' as they used to say. A good number of them were Whigs, who worshiped Henry Clay, and who favored staying *in* the Union."

"Yes, Lord," said Captain Dix. "It was an incredibly wealthy town, before the war. The land around here is very rich and productive. And Natchez was full of millionaires. It was nicknamed 'the Saratoga of the South,' after the wealthy spa in the North. I've heard there were more millionaires living here in Natchez than you could find in any other town in the Union, with the exception of New York City."

"Numerous, but *misguided* millionaires, nevertheless," said Pa. "I reckon most of them are as poor as Job's turkey, today!"

Everybody laughed at that. Then Pa got started talking, as he often does, about how wrong slavery had been, and how sinful the rebellion was. And he ended up quoting from

Captain John Cannon

In Natchez

the Bible about how it was supposed to be easier for a camel to pass through the eye of a needle, than for a rich man to get into heaven. I believe he's right in what he says, too.

While they were talking, our carriage was passing beneath crepe myrtle and live oak trees, on Pearl Street. Captain Dix pointed out to us the house where Captain Tom Leathers used to live before the war. It had a big, wide front gallery, and he called it Myrtle Terrace.

"Leathers lives in New Orleans, now, because his wife, Miss Charlotte, prefers it that way. But his sons, Bolling,

Captain Tom Leathers

Willie Jasper's Golden Eagle

and Tom, Jr., were born here. And so was his pretty little daughter, Courtney."

The men began talking about Captain Tom again.

"He must dress out at 270 pounds," said Mr. Samuels. "He stands six feet four inches in his stocking feet. Built like a bear. And he can blister the paint off the hurricane deck when he starts cussin'!"

"I declare I wish *I* could cuss like Captain Tom!" said Captain Dix, with real reverence in his voice. "I just wish I could come *near* him in that department, and that's a fact!"

We decided to end our tour of the town, because the sun was beginning to set. So we went over to the Mansion House, and I had some ice-cold sarsaparilla, while the men had mint juleps, served in frosted silver goblets.

While we were drinking on the gallery, waiting for supper to be served in the hotel, Captain Dix told Pa and Mr. Samuels and me a funny story about Kentucky men long ago in New Orleans. It was a story stretching way back fifty years or more, back to the time when General Andrew Jackson went down there, in 1815, to fight the British.

Pa said he'd take me down to Chalmette, just south of New Orleans, when we arrived, to show me where Jackson fought and won that battle in the War of 1812.

Louisiana had only been in the Union about a dozen years back then, at the time of Andy Jackson and the Battle of New Orleans. So those old French Creoles weren't very friendly to the backwoods folk who'd come downriver from Kentucky, with their coonskin caps, and their smooth-bore rifles, and their back-country ways.

In fact, the French there would watch them whooping and hollering and getting drunk, and they'd call them "mauvais Kaintuck." Captain Dix said that was French for "rotten Kentuckians."

In Natchez

But Captain Dix said the men from Kentucky had a name for the French that was *almost* just as bad. They called those Creoles "damned Kiskydees."

Well, you know why they said that? Because the French in New Orleans couldn't speak any English, and when the Kentucky men would say something to them, the French would ask each other:

"*Qu'est-ce qu'il dit? Qu'est-ce qu'il dit?*" (That means: "What did he say?")

And in French that sounds almost *exactly* like "Kiskydee?" Because those Creoles can talk French real *fast*.

We had a great big supper at the Mansion House, and then we walked back down the Natchez bluff in the moonlight, to the place where the *Creole Belle* was tied up to the bank, next to the Natchez wharfboat.

I heard the ladies who had gone to Brown's Gardens come back, talking about the camellias they'd seen—pretty pink and white and red flowers, growing on huge bushes. Those camellias had fancy names, like Gloire de Nantes, and Pink Perfection, and Governor Mouton, and Opelousas Peony.

Before Pa and I went to bed, Captain Dix told us that we'd probably make New Orleans late the following evening.

Down "The Coast"

We left Natchez real early the next morning and started downriver in the *Creole Belle*. It was June 19, 1870. (I'll put down later on how come I happened to be so sure of the date.)

I watched the roustabouts rolling barrels of molasses on board and listened to them singing while they loaded coal.

Here's the way their song went:

> On the levee by the riverside
> I've left my girl in New Orleans . . .
> She is young, just in her teens,
> On the levee by the riverside.

A boy just about my age came up the gangplank with a man I figured was probably his pa. It didn't take me long to learn that his name was Dennis Fallon, and that Mr. Fallon, his father, was a salesman for a carpet company located in Cincinnati. I told him all about me and Pa going to New Orleans, too.

Down "The Coast"

When the *Creole Belle* got under way, Dennis and I went down to the main deck to watch the men in the engine room stoke the boilers with coal and pine logs. They told us that when Captain Dix wanted to send up real black columns of smoke, he'd order them to throw in barrels of tar! And, if he wanted a sudden burst of speed, he'd call for a couple of tubs of lard, or maybe even a side of bacon, to be flung into the fire.

I don't think he asked for lard very often, though. Because I knew from what Mr. Samuels had told me, that the "old mud turtle's boilers" weren't nearly so strong as they once were.

Officers of a riverboat

After that, Dennis and I walked up front to talk to the roustabouts who were lying about on deck. One of them, a huge black fellow named Goliath, threw a pinch of tobacco overboard and tried to make us boys believe he'd done that as a present for Old Al.

"And who's Old Al supposed to be?" said Dennis.

"You ain't never heard of Old Al?" Goliath laughs. "He's just the biggest alligator in the river, that's who. *King* of the alligators, he is. Old Al can make a meal of both you boys, before either one of you could bat an eye. And if he give the *Creole Belle* one lick with his tail, he'll sink her down to the bottom of the river!"

Goliath tried to make us believe that Old Al wore a gold crown and smoked a pipe so hard that he could make a fog come up over the river. He told us Old Al could heave up sandbars right under a ship, if he wanted to. But Dennis and I weren't fooled by Goliath's stories. There have been plenty of ships to blow up on this river, and plenty sunk by rocks and snags and sawyers, and plenty more burnt up by sparks from their own smokestacks. But it wasn't any Old Al who was to blame!

Around the middle of the afternoon, Mr. Samuels asked me and Dennis if we wanted to come up and stand beside him in the pilothouse. Of course we said yes.

That's how we happened to be there, looking south down the river, when we got our first sight of the *Natchez*.

She'd left New Orleans that morning, and Mr. Samuels kind of smiled at me when I started showing off and told Dennis that the *Natchez* was trying to break the record between New Orleans and St. Louis, set twenty-six years ago by the *J. M. White*.

"Never you mind him, Dennis," said Mr. Samuels. "*I* told

him that's what the *Natchez* was fixing to do, just a few days ago, myself. Just you ask Willie Jasper what that record *was* that the *J. M. White* set, and we'll see how smart he is."

"Well, what *was* it?" said Dennis.

I surprised him and Mr. Samuels when I shot back: "Three days, twenty-three hours, and nine minutes."

They didn't think I could remember!

I wish you could have seen the *Natchez* storming along, throwing up a curved jet of spray thirty feet ahead of her bow. Her engines were throbbing and the river was churned up by her huge paddle wheels.

"Just one inch shy of forty-three feet in diameter," said Mr. Samuels, when we asked him how big they were.

Her smokestacks were painted bright red, and each one had "Natchez" lettered on two sides of it, way up at the top. And both wheelhouses had a big "Natchez" painted on the side—so big that you could read the letters about a mile away. Between her stacks, they had a gilded cotton bale strung up, made of tin, I reckon.

Captain Dix saluted the *Natchez* with the *Creole Belle*'s steam whistle, and here come a big, deep, single-toned rumble back from Captain Leathers on the *Natchez,* in answer. She was really thundering along, and we rocked and bounced on the big waves she threw up when she passed us.

Mr. Samuels said she was mighty fast.

"She's over three hundred feet long and she has eight boilers. And I wouldn't be surprised if she *does* take the horns to St. Louis, this time," said he.

Then he told me and Dennis that the roustabouts on board her call her "the big Injun," because Captain Leathers has a picture of this old Indian, named Pushmataha, worked out in stained glass up in the skylight over the main cabin.

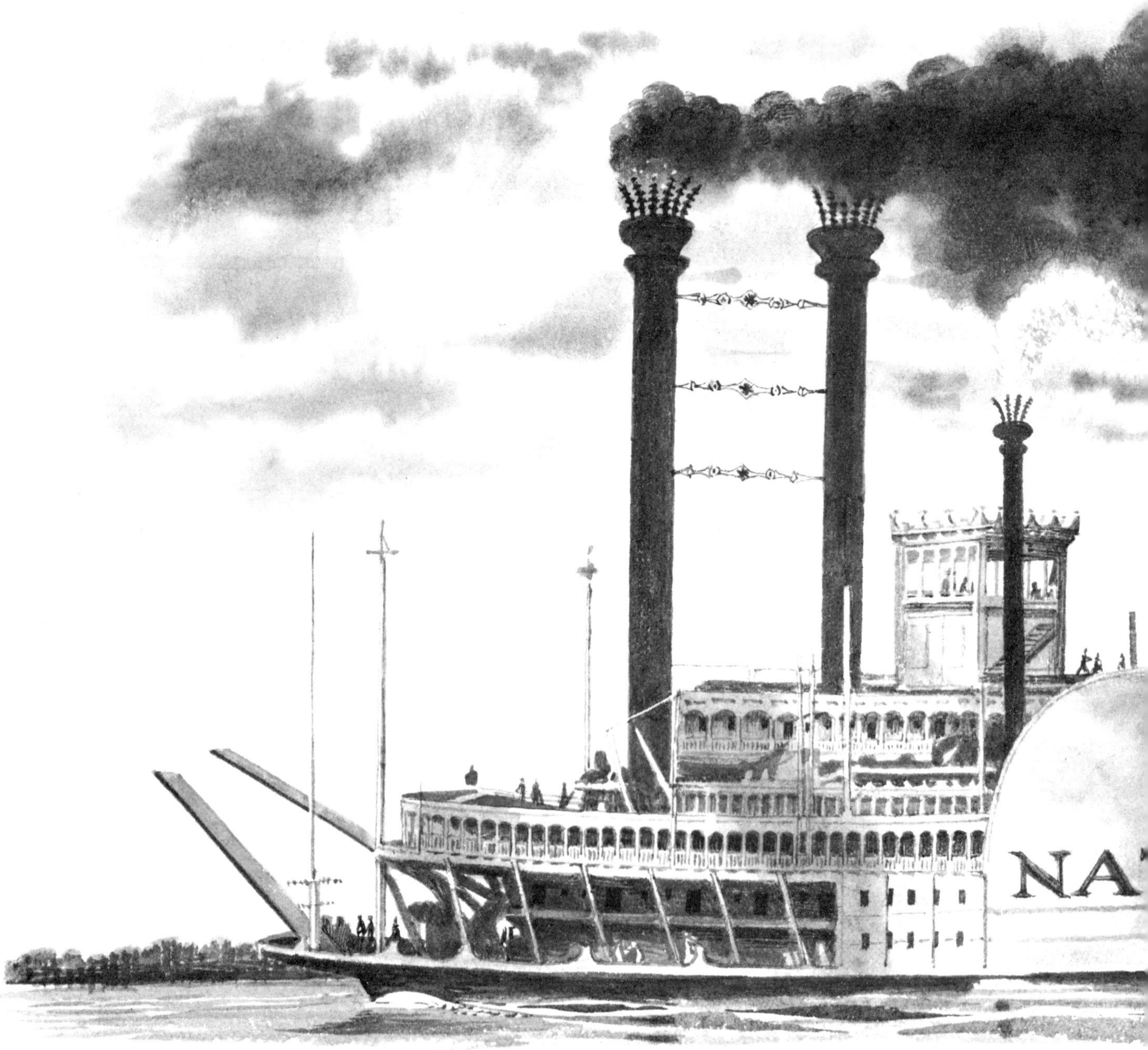
NAT

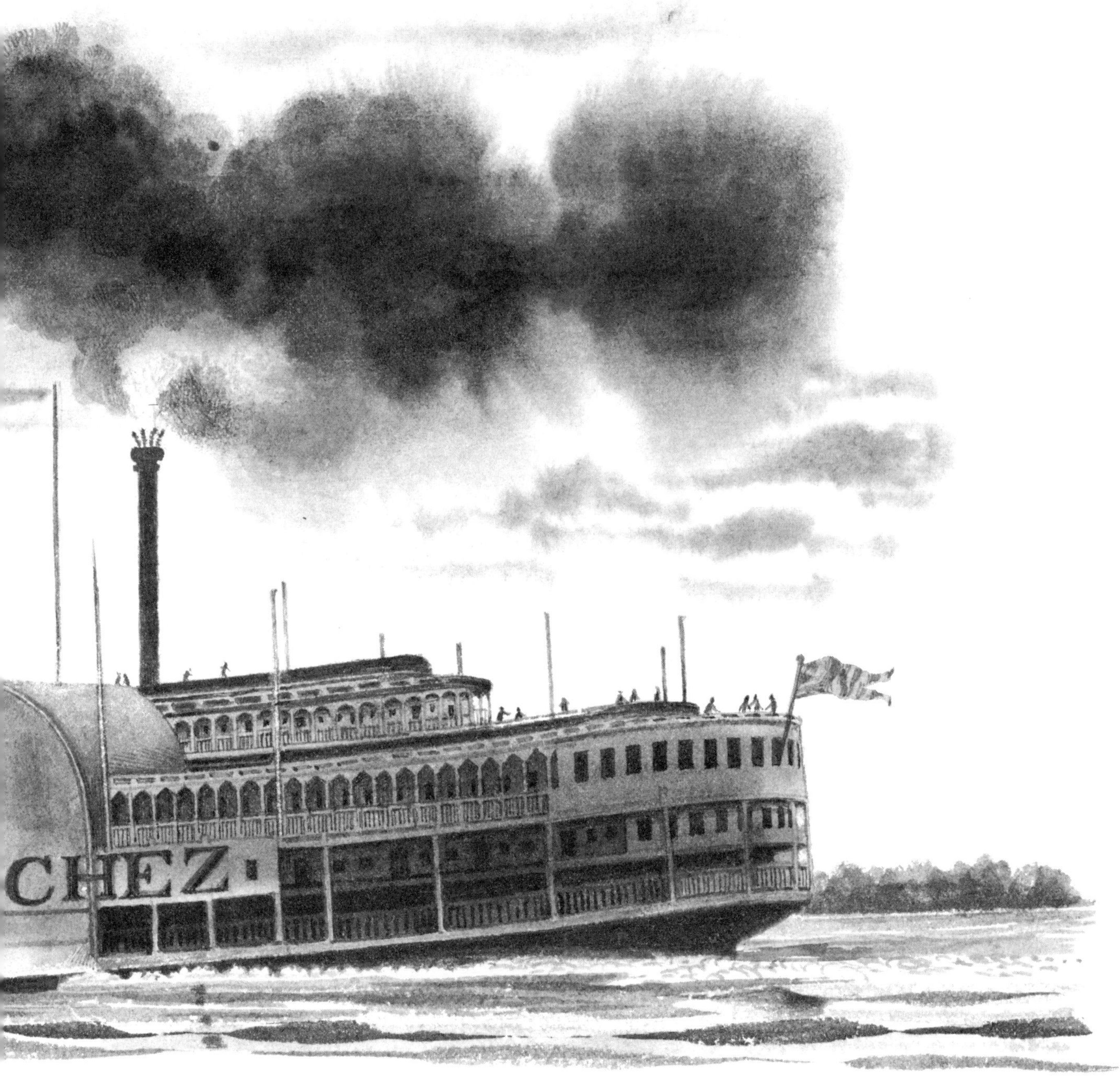
CHEZ

Willie Jasper's Golden Eagle

"I've even heard tell," said Mr. Samuels, "that Cap'n Leathers has been known to have that old Pushmataha painted on the outside of the pilothouse—with his tomahawk upraised—when he's racing."

"I didn't see any Indian painted up there today," said Dennis.

"I believe you," said Mr. Samuels, spitting into his cuspidor. "I didn't see one myself. But everybody on the river calls Leathers 'Old Push,' for a nickname. And that's on account of Pushmataha, that's for sure."

Mr. Samuels told us that the real Pushmataha had been a Choctaw chief, and that all his people were forced out of Mississippi, over to Oklahoma, about thirty, forty years ago, when all the planters in Mississippi was crazy to grab up every scrap of land the Indians owned and turn it all into

Pushmataha, from the Natchez

cotton. The old chief himself had died a few years before that had happened, when he went to Washington, D.C., to visit the President.

"*Natchez* sure looks like the fastest on the river to *me*," I said.

Dennis spoke up then, and said, "My pa says the *Robert E. Lee* is faster!"

"No, she ain't either," I answered. And Dennis kept talking back and saying I was wrong until I thought about poking him in the eye. But I didn't do it, for fear Mr. Samuels would make me leave the pilothouse if I did. Then I thought of betting him ten dollars that I was right, but when I reached into my pocket, my golden eagle felt so good, I figured I didn't want to chance losing it just on Dennis' account. So I shut up.

After supper, we boys went back up into the pilothouse again. We'd passed the city of Baton Rouge around two in the afternoon, just before we'd caught sight of the *Natchez*. And from there to New Orleans, everything on both sides of the river was flat, flat, flat! Most of the names are French, too, from there on down. First there's Fausse Rivière, and then Manchac Point and Bayou Iberville and Bayou Goula and Bonnet Carré.

"All this big stretch in here is where all the big sugar plantations used to be, before the war," said Captain Dix.

"They call this, along here, 'The Coast,'" said Mr. Samuels. "All between Baton Rouge and New Orleans. And they still grow a world of sugar, even though it's not anything like what it used to be. See that fine-looking old place?

(Overleaf) *Sugar plantations on the Mississippi "coast"*

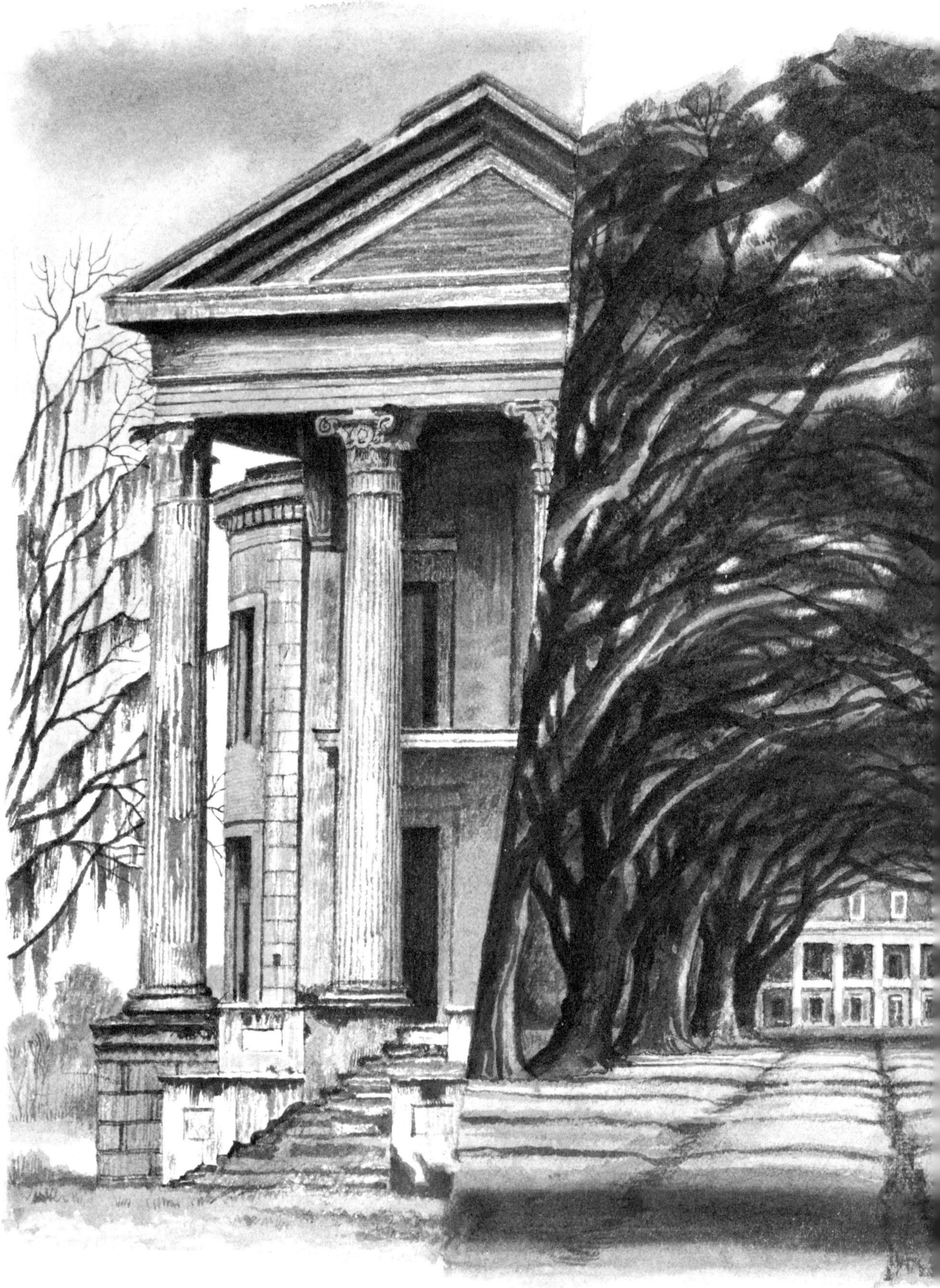

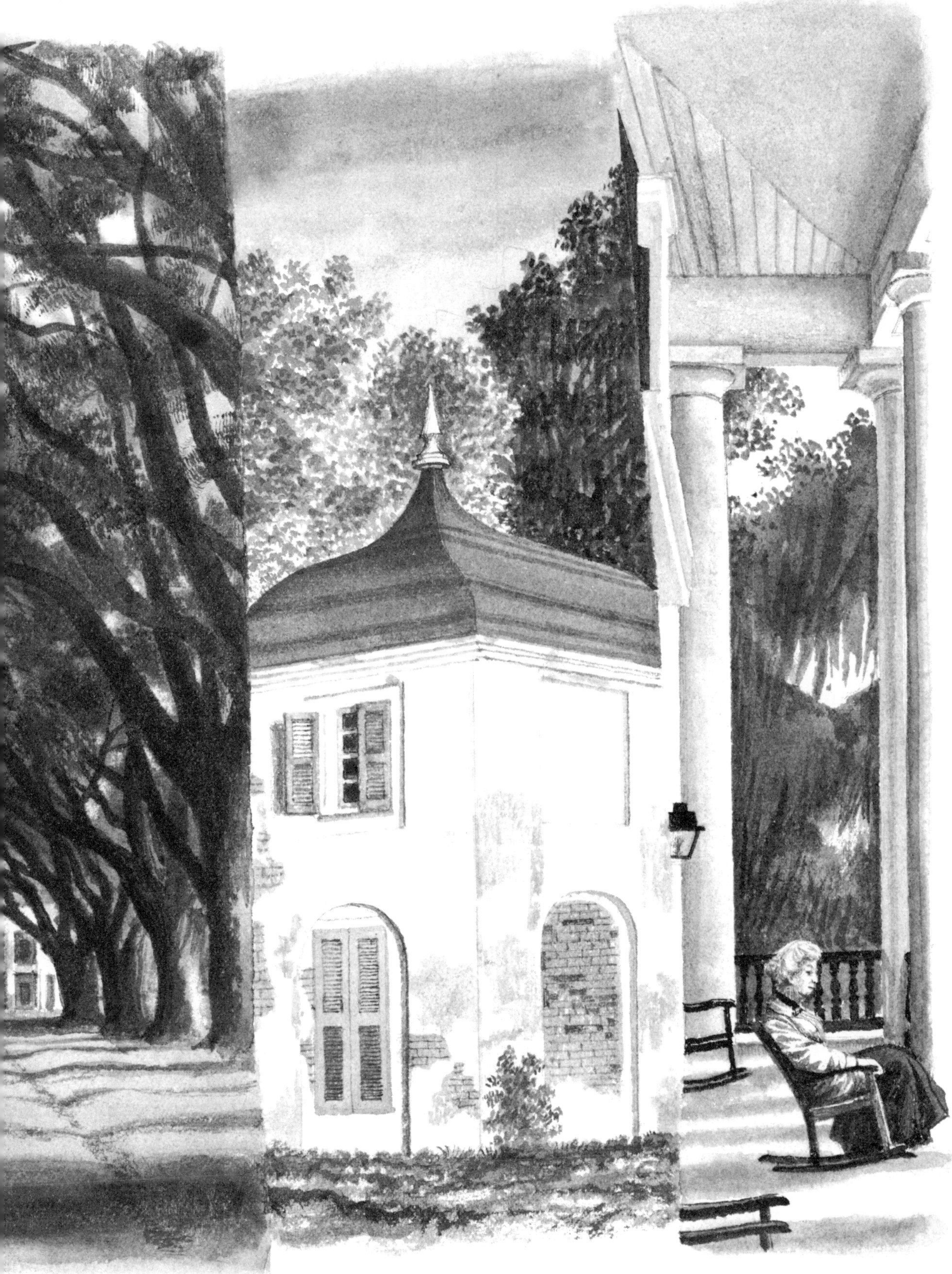

Willie Jasper's Golden Eagle

That's called Oak Alley. That's one of the grandest of them."

There, in the evening moonlight, at the end of a half mile of spreading, arching live oak trees, we boys could see the big old house. It had tall columns, two stories high, all around it. There was eight pillars across the front, and huge flowering vines climbing up all over the galleries.

"In the spring floods, down along here," said Mr. Samuels, "the river sometimes spreads thirty, forty miles wide over her banks. So wide a pilot can hardly tell where the channel is supposed to be."

Then he told us that the sugar cane was planted in July and August, and cut between October and January.

"After they grind the cane, and get the juice out of the stalks, they start big fires under the vats where the molasses is. They use the dry stalks to feed the fire, where they're making sugar. They call that dried cane the *bagasse*. That's a French word. And when you come through here in January, with all those fires going, you think you're approaching the entrance to hell. Columns of black smoke going up every way you look. But in the old days, before the war, if you had one or two good years, you'd have your fortune made for life, in sugar. It wasn't anything to clear $50,000 in a good year...."

Dennis and me must have got sleepy listening to Mr. Samuels talking about pink buttercups and white herons with black legs and yellow bills, and other things you could see in the cane fields. That and everything else he knew about the old days "before the war." I must have gone to sleep while he was still talking, because I don't remember going to bed at all.

When I woke up in my stateroom the next morning, we was tied up at the levee in New Orleans, and Pa told me we'd been there since eleven o'clock the night before.

My Big Mistake

New Orleans, the "Crescent City," was the place where I made my big mistake. And I made it when I let Dennis Fallon get me mad. But this isn't the place to get into that, so I'll just save it for later.

Pa sure spent a world of time and money taking me around New Orleans and showing me things.

Soon as we got up that first morning, Pa showed me the *batture,* which is what they call the river side of the levee. Since it was June, and the river was real low, we couldn't see the town from the boiler deck of the *Creole Belle.* But he told me that when the river is in flood, in April, the water comes right up to the top of the levee, nearly, and from the lowest deck of a packet on the river you can look right down into the town, because then you're sitting way up *higher* than New Orleans itself. That must be a strange feeling.

Anyway, a lot of the street names there are in French, because New Orleans used to belong to France, until the United States bought it, back in 1803. There's Chartres Street, and Royal Street, and Iberville Street, and Poydras

Willie Jasper's Golden Eagle

Street, and names like that. We stayed at the St. Charles Hotel, and Dennis Fallon and Mr. Fallon stayed there, too.

First day we were in New Orleans, Pa took me and Dennis down to Chalmette, just south of the city, like he'd promised, to show us where General Andrew Jackson and his soldiers fought and stopped the British, along the canal, there, when they were trying to capture New Orleans in 1815.

We had supper that night—Pa and me and Dennis and Mr. Fallon—at Cassidy's Restaurant, on Gravier Street, opposite our hotel. The men must have eaten three dozen raw oysters apiece! Dennis and I ate a dozen each ourselves. It was a real good supper, and when it was over, Mr. Fallon wanted to flip a coin with Pa, to see who was going to pay the bill. Mr. Fallon lost.

Later, when we was alone, Pa said to me, "Willie, I don't believe in gambling like that, you know, but I didn't want that fellow to think I was too stingy to pay for dinner. And that's why I let him do it, since he wanted it that way."

Pa sure hates gambling. He's always telling me money's too hard to earn to gamble it away.

But from what I could see, there was an awful lot of people down in New Orleans who felt different about that subject than Pa did! That's *some* gambling town.

The next day Pa was busy with his business affairs all morning, so I went past the warehouses on Decatur Street, and down Canal Street to the river, where all the packets are lined up at the bank, along the levee, just like they are at St. Louis.

Then I walked back to the French Quarter, where I saw the big new U. S. Customs House, and all those lacy iron balconies they got on the front of most of the buildings there, and the shady arcades you walk under along most of

A street in New Orleans

Willie Jasper's Golden Eagle

those narrow streets. The windows of the upper stories have long green blinds they call "jalousies," shut up tight against the sun. And there's lots of flowering trees and bushes, and the air is kind of wet and hot and heavy with heat and perfume, both. Back behind many a house you can see courtyards and walled gardens with palm trees and a spikey plant, called Spanish daggers, and flowering vines.

Pa took me one night to hear Madame Adelina Patti sing an opera called *The Barber of Seville.* I didn't understand much of it, but the music was pretty.

And another night, he took me and Dennis to see Mr. Joe Jefferson, in a play called *Rip van Winkle,* about a man who falls asleep for fifty years, or some long time, anyway (I forget just how long it was) and comes back home to find his wife dead and his family grown up long since. Dennis and me thought Joe Jefferson was a mighty fine actor. So did Pa.

Four days after we got to New Orleans, we read in the *Picayune*—that's their newspaper—that Captain Tom Leathers had broke the record of the *J. M. White,* and won the horns for the *Natchez* on his trip upriver to St. Louis.

"Made it to St. Louis yesterday morning, June 22, in three days, twenty-one hours, and fifty-eight minutes," said Pa. "One hour and eleven minutes better than the old record!"

I sure looked forward to telling *that* piece of news to Dennis Fallon. Smart aleck! I *told* him the *Natchez* was fast!

In the paper that morning there was another article talking about Captain Cannon of the *Robert E. Lee.* Seems the reporters up in Cairo asked him if he'd read about the *Natchez's* new record-breaking run to St. Louis, and he said of course he'd read of it, but he thought the *Lee* could do better. The article said the *Natchez* was due back in New

My Big Mistake

Orleans in another few days, and Cannon was going to be in New Orleans himself, on the *Lee,* before long. Cannon had already sent out notice that the *Lee* was going to be starting upriver again, on Thursday, June 30, on her regular announced run to Louisville, Kentucky.

The smart-aleck Cairo reporter had gone on to tell Cannon that he'd heard that Captain Tom Leathers planned to leave New Orleans on the *Natchez* at *exactly* the same time —5:00 P.M., on June 30—and what did Captain Cannon think of that?

Pa read all of this to me from the paper. And what Captain Cannon answered the reporter was this: that *he* was making a regular business trip on the *Lee,* and that he *wasn't* racing. But he added if the *Natchez* tried to pass the *Lee* on the river, the *Lee* would do everything possible to prevent it. And he said the *Natchez* would think the *Lee* was "a hundred miles long" before she got entirely past.

Pa really laughed when he read that.

"Such foolishness!" he said, throwing down the paper, as he got ready to shave. "Both Cannon and Leathers know how dangerous racing is, so both of 'em have to say they're *not* planning to race, you see. But both of 'em getting ready for a race, just as hard as they can."

I didn't see how Pa could be so certain there *was* going to be a race, until a couple of days later, when, in the *Picayune* again, we read these two notices, printed side by side.

Here's what Captain Cannon of the *Lee* said:

A CARD

REPORTS HAVNG BEEN CIRCULATED THAT STEAMER *R. E. Lee* LEAVING FOR LOUISVILLE ON THE 30TH JUNE, IS GOING OUT FOR A RACE, SUCH REPORTS

ARE NOT TRUE, AND THE TRAVELLING COMMUNITY ARE ASSURED THAT EVERY ATTENTION WILL BE GIVEN TO THE SAFETY AND COMFORT OF PASSENGERS.

THE RUNNING AND MANAGEMENT OF THE *Lee* WILL IN NO MANNER BE AFFECTED BY THE DEPARTURE OF OTHER BOATS.

JOHN W. CANNON, MASTER.

And here's what Captain Leathers, of the *Natchez,* had to say:

A CARD TO THE PUBLIC

BEING SATISFIED THAT THE STEAMER *Natchez* HAS A REPUTATION OF BEING FAST, I TAKE THIS METHOD OF INFORMING THE REPUBLIC THAT THE REPORTS OF THE *Natchez* LEAVING HERE NEXT THURSDAY, THE 30TH INST., INTENDING RACING, ARE NOT TRUE. ALL PASSENGERS AND SHIPPERS CAN REST ASSURED THAT THE *Natchez* WILL NOT RACE WITH ANY BOAT THAT WILL LEAVE HERE ON THE SAME DAY WITH HER. ALL BUSINESS ENTRUSTED TO MY CARE WILL HAVE THE BEST ATTENTION.

T. P. LEATHERS,
MASTER, STEAMER *Natchez.*

"Now, Willie, my boy," said Pa, with a short laugh, "you're never going to have better proof than *that*. If those

My Big Mistake

two denials don't add up to convince you there's going to be a race next Thursday, then that's because you come from so deep in the state of Missouri that you won't believe the sun will come up in the east, until you *see* it."

I told Pa I took his meaning. Everybody else in New Orleans must have felt the way we did, too. Because everywhere we went that morning people were betting on who was going to win—the *Natchez* or the *Robert E. Lee.*

Not just in New Orleans, either. The following day we read in the *Picayune* that folks had commenced betting in St. Louis, and Cincinnati, and New York, and all over the United States. Even as far off as London and Paris, way off in Europe! The whole *world* seemed to know the race was coming, and everyone was interested.

Of course, I was interested, too. And that's where I made my big mistake. Because Pa and Mr. Fallon took Dennis and me to have a look at the cathedral, that day, over on Jackson Square. And after that, we went into the Cabildo, the building next door to the church, where the Spanish and the French used to govern Louisiana, way back when they owned it.

We talked about the race, and naturally, Dennis Fallon said the *Lee* was going to win. He said he hoped his Pa would take him back up to St. Louis on Captain Cannon's ship.

I couldn't let Pa hear what I said, because I know he hates betting. But I got so mad at Dennis Fallon, I lowered my voice and said: "Look, boy, you don't know what you're talking about. The *Natchez* is going to whip the *Lee* so bad, it's going to be like the Yanks and the Rebels all over again!"

"Says who?" said Dennis. "Says who, Willie Jasper?"

"Here's *ten dollars* says so," I said, hauling my gold eagle out of my pocket.

Willie Jasper's Golden Eagle

Well, for a minute Dennis Fallon just gawps at my money. Then he says:

"I'll take that bet, Willie Jasper. And I'll take that money, too. You see if I don't."

Then we shook on it. And Mr. Fallon went off somewhere with Pa for a drink of absinthe, and he give Dennis a quarter to treat me to ice cream.

After we had our ice cream, I went on back to the hotel. I was sore at Dennis for having made me so mad I'd gone and bet my money. It was a foolish thing he made me do, and I was mad at him for it. And mad at myself even more than at him.

The clerk in the hotel lobby gave me a letter for Pa. It was from Alton, and I recognized Mamma's handwriting.

It wasn't too long before Pa came back. He opened the letter, and read it, frowning.

"Doctor says—I mean to say, your Mamma says she's lonesome for us, Willie, and why don't we head for home real soon."

I reckon Mamma told Pa that the doctor said the baby was due any time. But Pa didn't want to put it that way to me, I guess, because I wasn't supposed to know about the baby at all. Grownups think we're real stupid, sometimes.

"I've had enough of New Orleans," I said.

"And I'm all done with what I came here to do," said Pa. "If I could get us passage on the *Natchez* for tomorrow afternoon, I reckon we might be home on the Fourth of July."

The Start of the Great Steamboat Race

I don't know how he did it, but Pa managed to get us passage on the *Natchez*. Early the next afternoon we went down to the levee right after dinner, even though the ship wasn't due to leave until five. We knew there'd be a huge crowd gathering to see the *Lee* and the *Natchez* shove off. The *Picayune* said there might be as many as ten thousand down there, and they were running special excursion boats for folks who wanted to watch the race from the river.

It's a lucky thing we left early, because the dray with our trunks could hardly get through all the carriages and wagons and crowds of people already jamming the bank. By three o'clock, we managed to see our baggage safely carried aboard. We had to fight our way through people selling candy and cake and gingerbread and some kind of little tarts they call "wharf pies." Seemed like everybody in New Orleans was down there, on the batture.

Willie Jasper's Golden Eagle

Once we got our stuff into our stateroom, I went looking for Dennis Fallon. I expected to find him on the *Lee*. And I did. And that's when we had our fight.

Pa and I had heard the odds folks were giving on the race, in favor of the *Lee*. It seems seventy-five dollars would get you a hundred dollars the *Natchez* was going to lose.

And that was because Captain Cannon wasn't playing it straight, and Captain Leathers was. Word had got out that Cannon wasn't carrying any freight at all. And he wasn't carrying but a few passengers, either. We heard he wasn't going to make any stops at all, this trip—for freight *or* passengers. He'd canceled his run to Louisville and was going straight up past Cairo to St. Louis. And furthermore, he'd taken out the windowglass of the *Lee*'s cabins and pilothouse, stripped his ship down every way he could think of, throwing out furniture and spare anchor chains and whatnot, so's to cut down on weight and wind resistance. Cannon was determined to win. Didn't care what he had to do, so long as he could beat the *Natchez*.

Well, Captain Leathers wasn't going to act that way. He refused to take any freight, just like Captain Cannon had done. But he didn't strip his ship down, and he had more than ninety passengers booked, and he planned to make all his regular stops at Natchez, Vicksburg, Greenville, Memphis, and Cairo, same as he always did.

Captain Leathers was naturally going to lose time if he had to make all those stops, and the *Lee* didn't. That's part of the reason I was so mad at Dennis. When I saw him, near the gangway of the *Lee*, I pushed through the roustabouts and all the crowd gathered there. And I said to him:

"Since you're not making any stops at all, maybe I should just hand over my gold eagle to you right now! No need to wait till St. Louis to see how this'll turn out!"

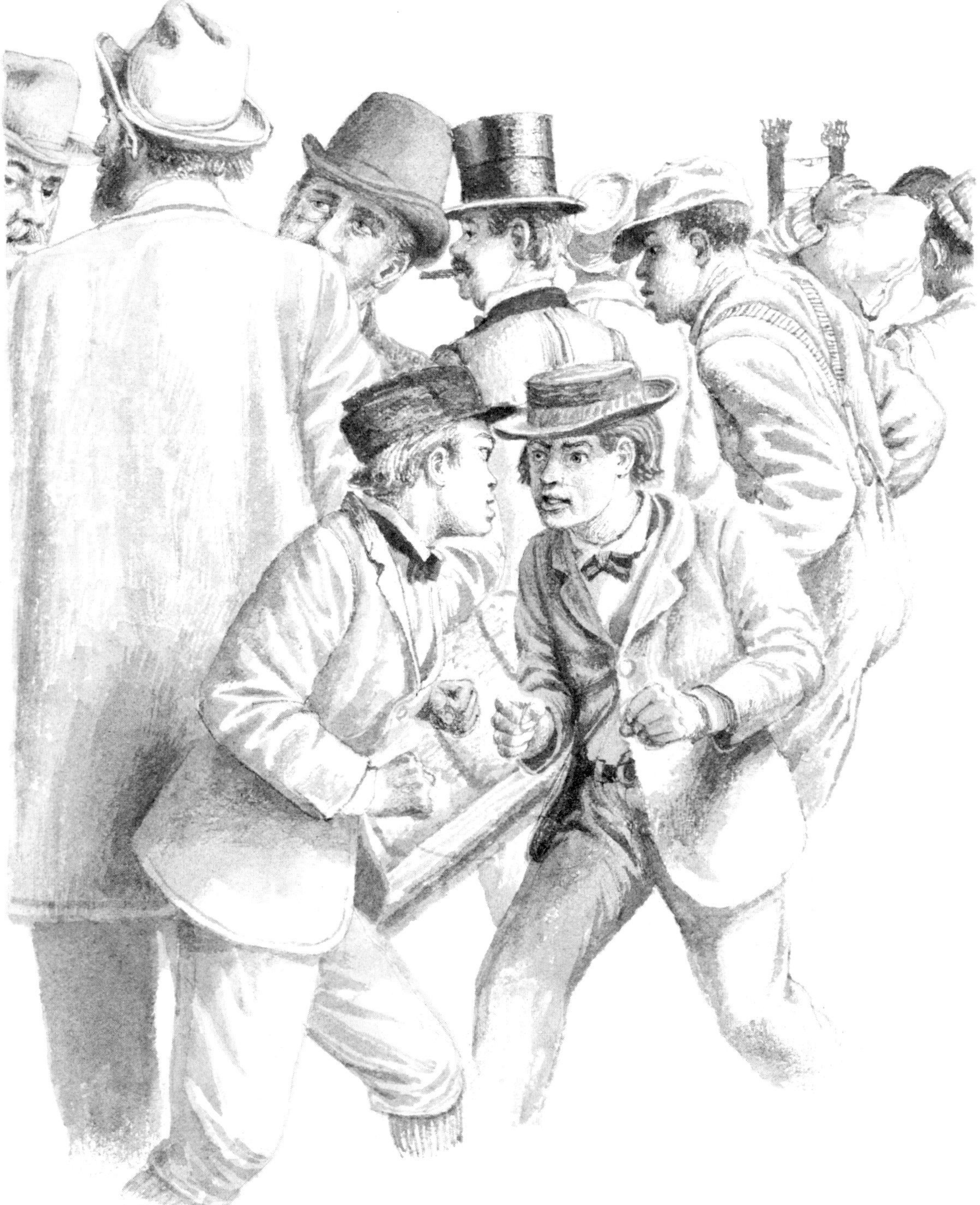

Willie Jasper's Golden Eagle

Dennis sure got mad when he heard that, and we both pitched in. Pretty soon he had a bloody nose, and my eye was sort of black by the time Mr. Fallon pulled us apart. Pa come up and he and Mr. Fallon shook hands.

"Well, boys *will* do it . . ." I heard Pa say. Neither one of the men seemed half as mad as Dennis and me was.

"Boys, hell!" said Mr. Fallon. "Captain Leathers and Captain Cannon have been known to do some scrapping themselves."

"So I've heard," said Pa. "They're supposed to have come to blows, here, a couple of years ago. And when they did, Cannon seems to have gotten the best of *that* one!"

I'd been hoping Mr. Fallon and Pa were going to fight, too, so's I could hit Dennis again. But no such luck. They made us boys shake hands. So me and Dennis *had* to do it. But I kept wishing I hadn't been such a fool as to bet my gold eagle on a race that didn't seem to be starting out fair.

It really never *was* fair, to my mind. First thing Captain Cannon did—he didn't wait till quite five o'clock to get started. He rang his bells and cut his hawsers, and backed out into the river, and headed north. Got the jump on all of us in the *Natchez*. People began hollering "Hurrah for the Hoppin' Bob!" That's what they'd nicknamed the *Robert E. Lee*.

Captain Tom Leathers was cussing and hollering. Bells rang, and the *Natchez* backed out into the river, in pursuit of the *Lee*—but we was better than three minutes behind her, starting off.

By 5:01 the *Lee* was churning past St. Mary's Market, at the foot of Canal Street. Bells were ringing and people were hollering like mad. Captain Cannon shot off his deck gun.

We weren't able to answer his starting gun with ours until *we* came up to Canal Street, ourselves. By then it was four

The Start of the Great Steamboat Race

and a half minutes past five! I felt in my pocket for my gold eagle. We already trailed them by three and a half minutes!

Somebody on board told Pa that Captain Cannon had the governor of Louisiana on board the *Robert E. Lee*. The governor's a fellow named Henry Clay Warmouth. He fought for the Union, as a colonel from Missouri. But, of course, the people down here call him a carpetbagger. (Well, he *is* a Republican, and if federal troops wasn't still occupying the state and supporting him at the polls, Pa says Warmouth never would have been elected.)

After we'd been grinding and pounding along for about an hour, we came upon a bunch of those excursion boats that had steamed up the river from New Orleans to see the start of the race. One of these was the *Mayflower*. Everybody on those boats was screaming and hollering for the *Lee* and the *Natchez,* both!

We learned, later, that up around Carrollton, the *Lee* had some trouble with one of her hot-water pipes—but her engineers patched her up, somehow, without stopping!

There were knots of people all along the levee watching the two boats race. It was dark by the time we got to Bonnet Carré Church, about forty miles above New Orleans. The *Natchez* was still lagging just a few minutes behind the *Lee*. They had bonfires burning on the levee there. It must have been around 7:30. People were still cheering both boats, just about equal it seemed to me, even though the *Natchez* was a couple of minutes behind.

We got to College Point, where Jefferson College is, just before 9:00 that night. Captain Leathers hadn't been seen in the main cabin at supper, and I couldn't eat much. I was worried. And the *Lee* seemed to keep about a mile ahead of us, every step of the way.

I hadn't told Pa I'd gone and bet my eagle on the race,

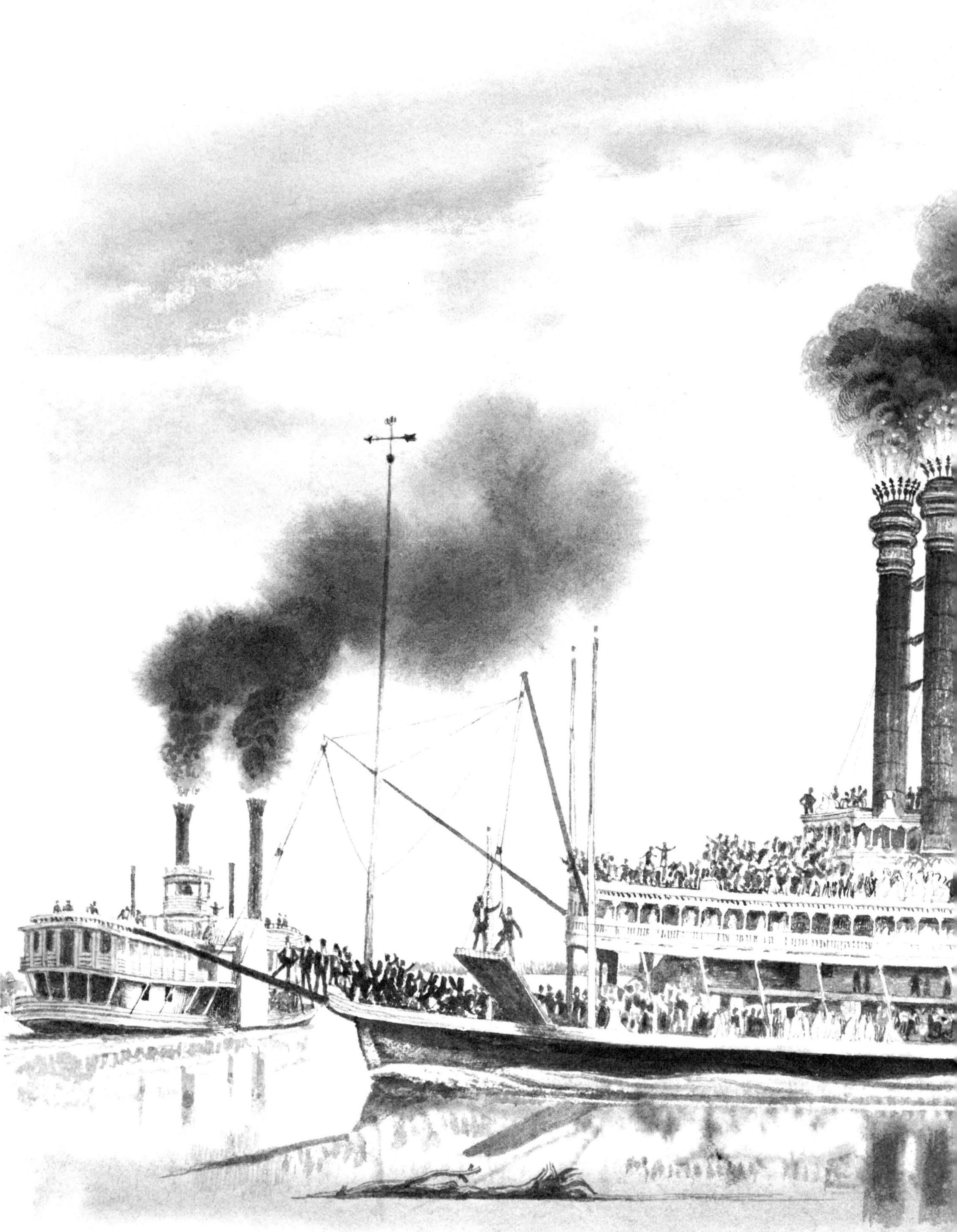

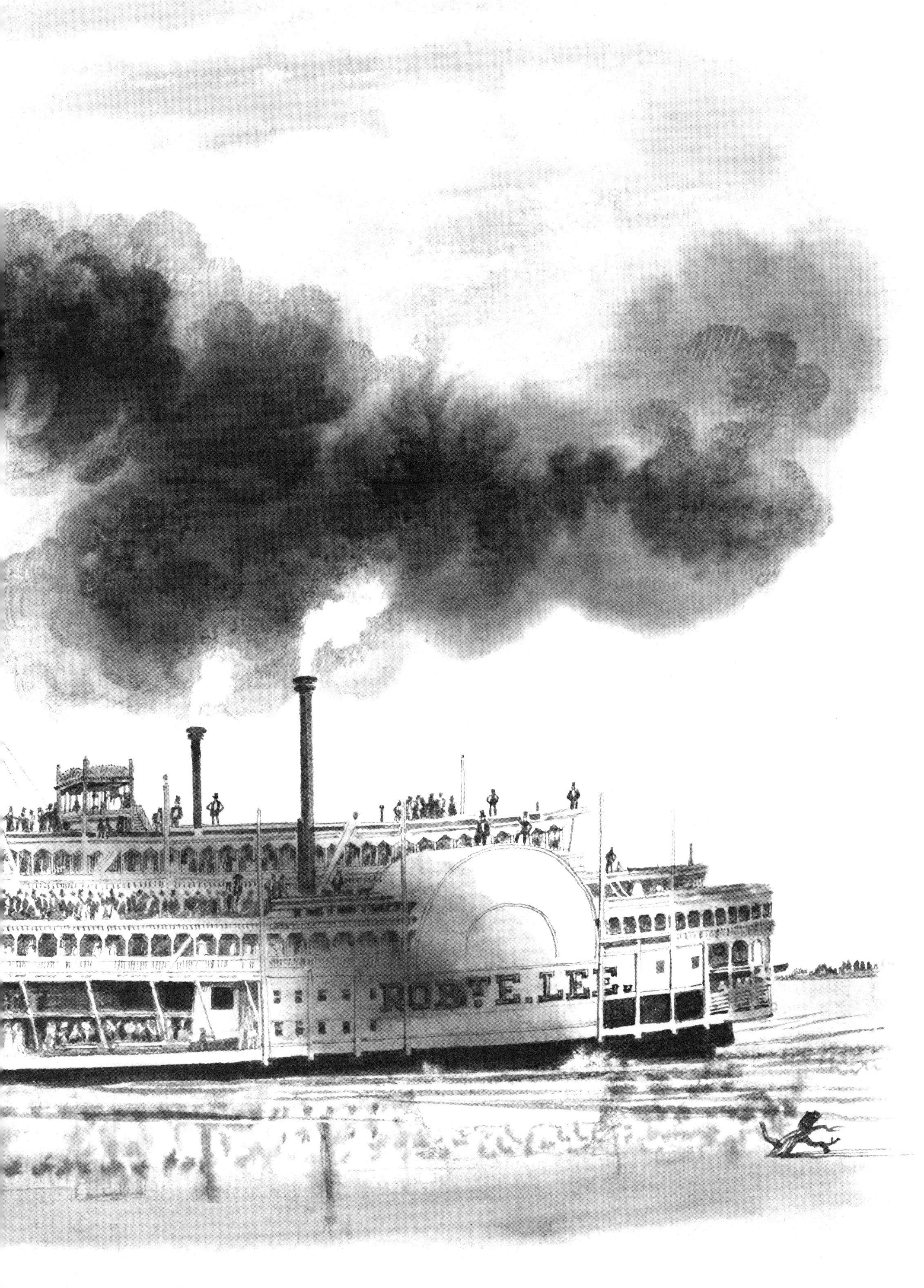
ROBT E. LEE

Willie Jasper's Golden Eagle

because I knew he would have laughed at me, or fussed, one or the other.

By eleven o'clock at night we had rounded Hampton Point and we was opposite Donaldsonville, seventy-eight miles above New Orleans.

About an hour later we got to St. Gabriel Church, at Hundred Mile Point, and there were more bonfires, and more crowds cheering both boats. But the *Lee* was still as far ahead of the *Natchez* as ever, and no matter how much our engines seemed to grind and pound, and no matter how much the ship shook and trembled, we never seemed to gain on her. The old Hoppin' Bob stayed up there, a mile ahead of us, and we rolled and wallowed in the wake of her waves.

Pa said Captain Leathers was down in the engine room, hollering and cussing at his firemen. We'd heard that the city of Natchez had given him some hams and fat meat to put in his furnaces—but whether he ever really burned them or not, Pa couldn't say.

I guess I must have went to sleep around then. Pa told me that we got to Plaquemine after midnight—about 113 miles above New Orleans—but you couldn't have proved it by me. I was dead to the world.

Next morning Pa told me we must have passed Baton Rouge around 3:00 in the morning, and Port Hudson and Bayou Sara a half hour later. In the very early hours of the morning we passed Racourcie Cutoff, where the Red River comes in. And, we heard, the *Natchez* had begun to gain a little on the *Lee* there. Not that I could tell you for sure. Because I was still asleep, and dreaming that I had Dennis Fallon up against a cotton bale, whaling the daylights out of him, for tricking me into betting ten dollars against him, on this fool steamboat race! A bet it sure began to look like I was going to lose.

What Happened at Natchez

Pa and I had a kind of dismal breakfast the next morning. I kept feeling my gold eagle in my pocket, and it was *there*, all right. But to me, it was just as good as gone. Might just as well already have been in Dennis Fallon's fist. Because way up there ahead of us was the smoke of the *Robert E. Lee*—and we didn't seem to be a bit closer to her than we had been the night before.

Coming downriver, on the *Creole Belle,* we'd stayed pretty much in the middle of the river, taking advantage of the current.

Going up, now, both the *Lee* and the *Natchez* was kind of hugging the bank, trying to *avoid* the current as much as possible. Sometimes we'd dart into chutes between islands and the bank. Chutes that we never would have dared attempt on the way down.

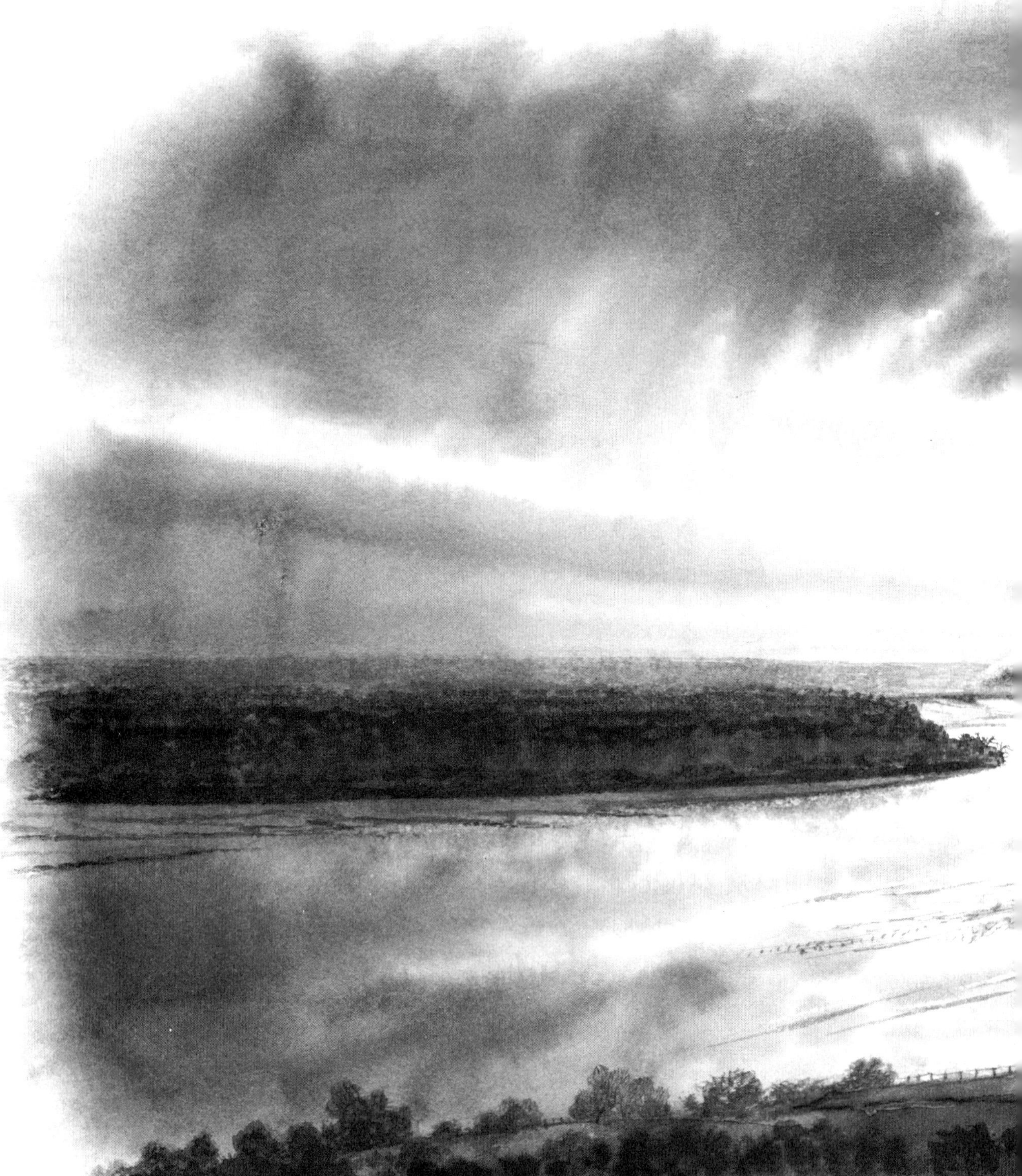

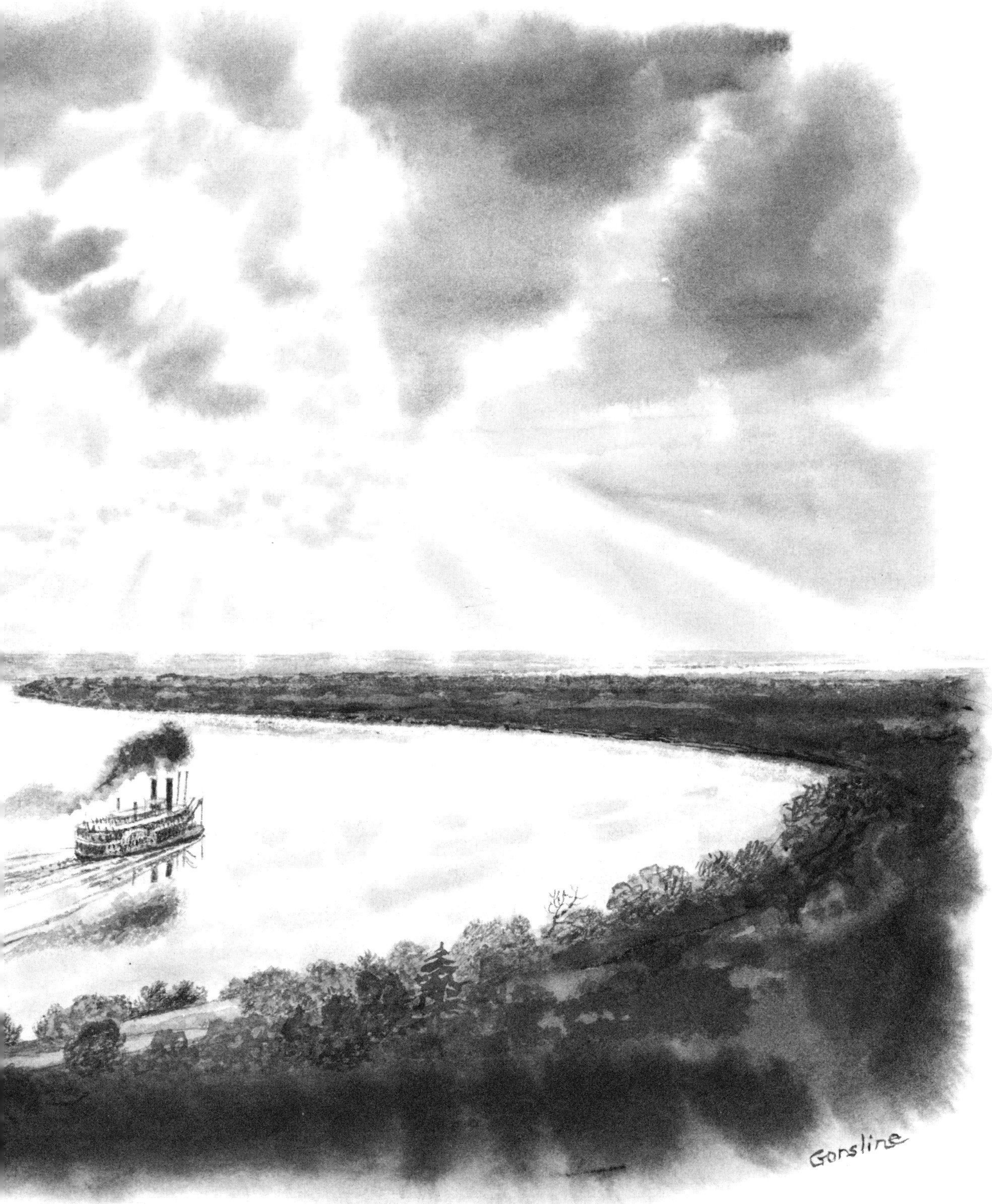
Gonsline

Willie Jasper's Golden Eagle

But it didn't seem to do the *Natchez* any good. The pilots on the *Lee* knew all those tricks, too. And we didn't seem to be getting any closer to her, no matter what we did. No matter how many chunks of fatback and sides of bacon Captain Leathers had thrown into the fire, and no matter how many barrels of turpentine or tar, we couldn't gain on the *Lee*. Her engines were stronger than ours, and we just couldn't close that gap.

We got up to Natchez around half-past ten in the morning —but the *Lee* was already chugging upriver, nearly out of sight when we got up to the town. Captain Cannon had arranged to have two coal barges waiting for him out in the middle of the river, so he wouldn't even have to stop. He just took those barges in tow for a mile or two, and had his roustabouts load coal, while he kept steaming upriver. He didn't lose any time at all.

When we docked at Natchez, we learned that Cannon had hollered over to the wharfboat: "Take down those horns!" And they sent them out to him, on one of the coal barges. For the fact was, he *had* beat the old record that Captain Tom Leathers had set fourteen years ago with the *Princess*. He'd beat it by nineteen minutes!

The gilded elk horns had been sitting there, on the wharfboat, waiting for him, festooned with red and white and green ribbons. And the tag was still there, saying: WHY DON'T YOU TAKE THE HORNS? Well, Cannon got them, because now they belonged to him!

As it happened, Captain Tom Leathers had beat his own record, too. Because he made it to Natchez six minutes after the *Lee*—which was thirteen minutes better than his old record, on the *Princess*. But that didn't mean anything *that* morning, because he was behind the *Lee*. Six minutes behind.

What Happened at Natchez

They'd had a band down there, at Natchez-under-the-Hill, on the wharfboat, ready to serenade Leathers, as soon as the *Natchez* hove in sight. But they was so disappointed when he come in second that they didn't want to play at all.

Up on top of the bluff they'd had all-night parties going on in some of the big houses—waiting for the ships to appear. We heard that—as soon as they saw the smoke downriver—lots of people rushed out onto the footbridge over the gulley, up there on top of the bluff. Straining to see if it was the *Lee* or the *Natchez* that was first.

Well, of course, it was the *Lee,* and all the people up on the bluff were disappointed. But so many folks had piled onto that bridge that it cracked and collapsed. Lucky nobody was killed.

I *must* say I admired Captain Tom Leathers. He tied up at the wharfboat in Natchez, just as if the race wasn't on his mind at all. And he discharged twelve passengers, in the regular way. And he lost about another six minutes there, because he was doing business as usual, like he and Cannon was supposed to.

Cannon had had his special coal barges waiting for him out in the river, to save time. And he'd already refused all passengers above New Orleans, so he wouldn't have to stop anywhere and lose time.

I could see that that was shrewd, since he wanted to win so bad.

But I sure did admire Captain Leathers for playing the game strictly by the rules, even if it did make it seem that —acting that way—he was going to lose, for sure.

And that meant I was going to lose my eagle, too.

Worse and Worse

That afternoon, Captain Leathers made a special stop at Grand Gulf, at 5:15, to pick up ten passengers—and he lost about nine minutes getting them and their stuff aboard.

We was fourteen minutes behind the *Lee* at Vicksburg, and the same story all over again. Captain Cannon had picked up a couple of coal barges he had waiting for him there, out in the river. He tied them alongside and just kept charging upstream while his roustabouts unloaded the coal.

And like I knew he would, Captain Leathers docked at Vicksburg to let off seventeen regular passengers—and he lost a little more time.

Even so, we was narrowing the distance, and had just begun to catch up a bit with the *Lee,* when our cold-water pump went dead, in Milliken's Bend. It took us thirty-three minutes to get the blessed thing working again, and by the time it was fixed, the *Lee* was out of sight.

It was nearly sunset, July 1. I could just picture Dennis

Worse and Worse

Fallon smirking back at us from the hurricane deck of the *Lee,* as we dropped out of sight. I just wished I could have punched him real hard. Just once.

But there was nothing I could do. So I ate my supper and got undressed in my stateroom. And just before I turned out the light I looked real hard at my gold eagle. The engines were making the ship tremble and jump with their pounding. But I had a feeling we was going to lose, just the same.

Pa and me woke up around sunrise the next morning, Saturday, July 2. I guess the quiet must have waked us, because we was tied up against the bank, in Greenville, Mississippi, about 530 miles north of New Orleans. And for the moment the engines was silent.

One of the ship's officers told Pa that the *Lee* was an *hour* ahead of us now. That was because we'd run aground, during the night, at Island No. 93, and lost some more time.

But that wasn't the worst we heard! We heard that Captain John W. Cannon had done something that made me think that he should have been disqualified from the race. No question about it.

During the night, about sixty miles below Greenville, near Island No. 89, it seems that Cannon had this other steam packet waiting for him in the middle of the river.

She was called the *Frank Pargoud,* and she was carrying a big load of pine knots for the *Robert E. Lee.* The two ships tied together and ran upstream while the roustabouts transferred the wood from the *Pargoud* to the *Lee.*

Some said the *Lee* got the advantage of the *Pargoud*'s engines while this was happening. Others said the *Pargoud* was a lot slower than the *Lee,* and that she really slowed the *Lee* down.

Pa and me decided that what Cannon had done didn't

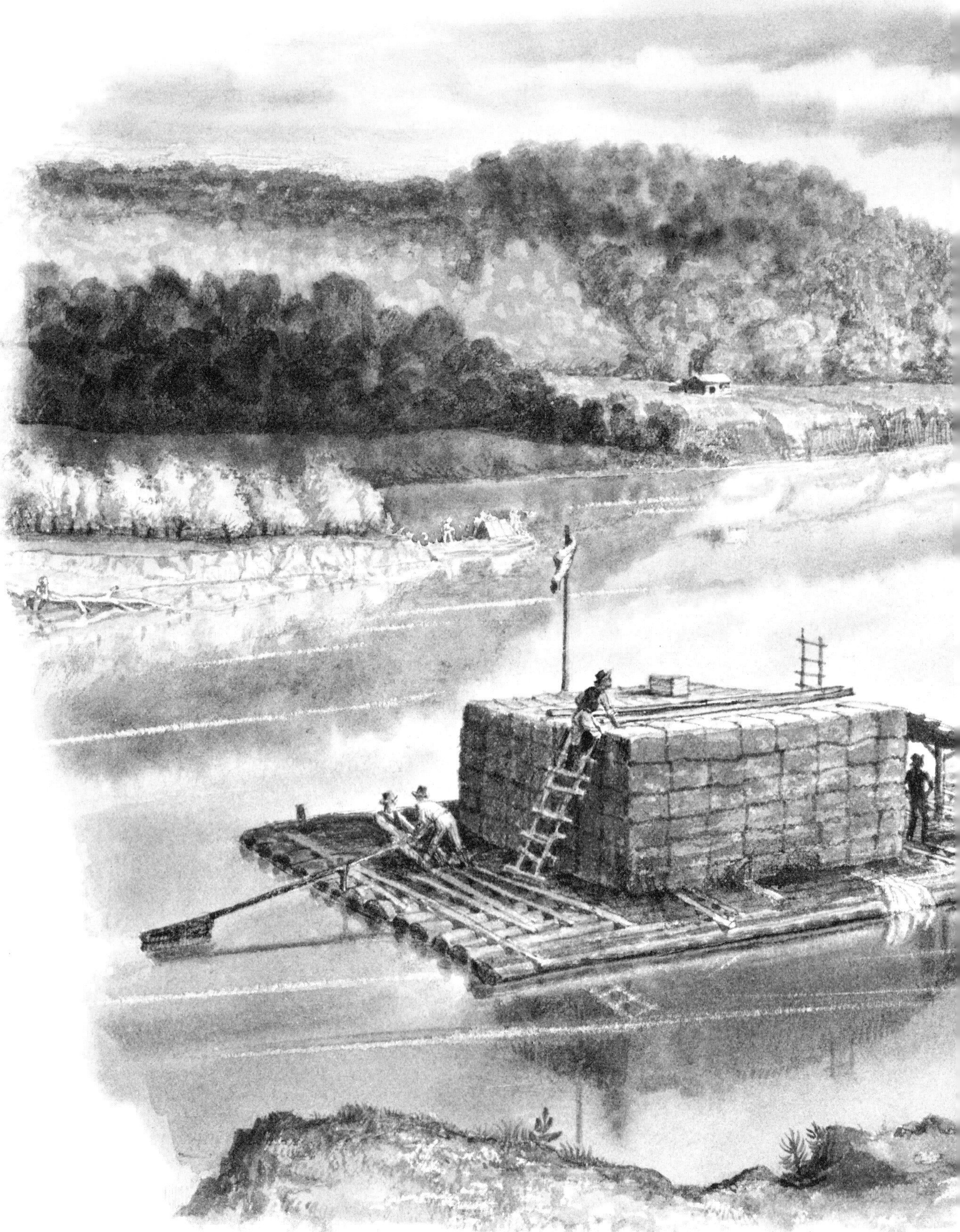

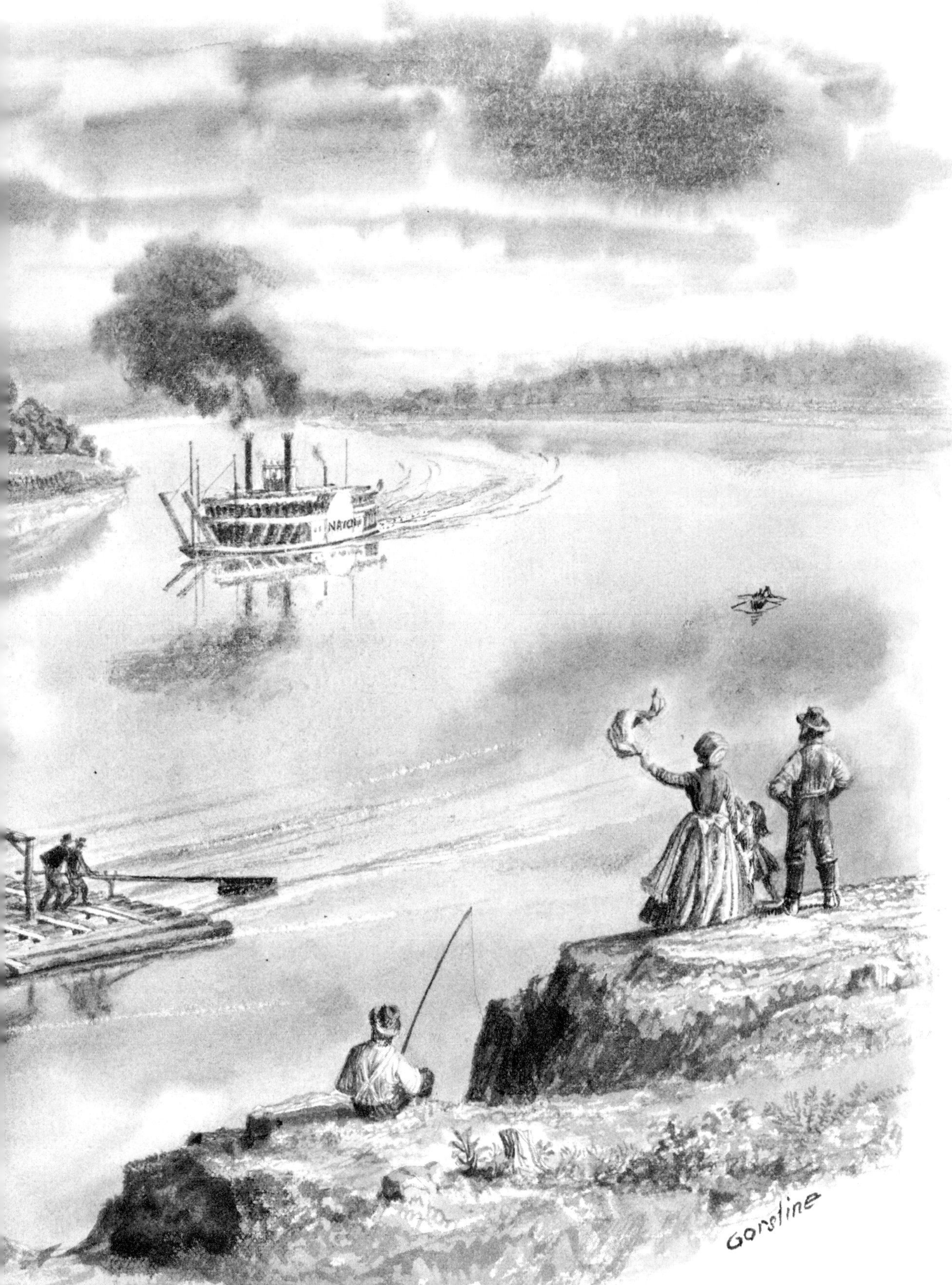
Gorstine

make the race fair and square any more. Because Captain Tom Leathers hadn't made any arrangements at all to have the *Natchez* refueled by ships waiting for him, out in the middle of the river.

"You think I have grounds to call off my bet, Pa?" I said.

"What bet is that, Willie?" said Pa.

And then I had to tell him I bet my gold eagle on the *Natchez*, against Dennis and the *Lee*. I was sorry I had to confess it.

Pa laughed. "If you got ten dollars to throw away gambling," he said, "you best learn to lose it like a man."

That wasn't the answer I wanted to hear. What Cannon was doing didn't seem fair to me, and I wished Pa could have understood *that* much. I didn't think he thought it was fair himself.

We heard Captain Leathers raging about what Cannon had done, with the *Frank Pargoud*, and all. Captain Tom was saying it was unlawful, and all bets above Vicksburg should be called off.

Well, folks may tell you it was a real exciting steamboat race and show you pictures of the two ships, racing along, neck and neck, as they say. But it wasn't like that at all, to my mind.

Up above Greenville, Mississippi, at Island No. 82, near Point Comfort, was the last glimpse any of us got of the *Robert E. Lee*. We saw her smokestacks disappearing around the point, twelve miles upriver, and we never saw her again until St. Louis!

Now, wouldn't that break your heart?

At Memphis, at midnight, or a few minutes after, in the early morning of Sunday July 3, we saw big bonfires and

Flatboatmen of the Mississippi

lots of people hollering and cheering for us. But we was trailing the *Lee* by one hour and three minutes!

Right above Memphis, amongst those islands called Paddy's Hen and Chickens, we run aground again, and lost some more time.

It's too dismal to keep on telling everything that went wrong. But late Sunday afternoon, July 3, it seems that Captain Cannon and his Hoppin' Bob pulled into Cairo at 5:49. The *Lee* had set a record, for she was exactly three days and one hour out of New Orleans. Naturally, everybody on the levee there must have cheered and hollered and hurrahed for Cannon.

I could imagine how good Dennis Fallon must have felt. But of course I didn't get a chance to *see* him. Because the *Natchez* didn't get to Cairo until one hour and eight minutes after the *Lee* had vanished upriver.

The Bitter End

Well, of course the *Natchez* lost. I'm ashamed to say by how much!

What happened was this: Sunday night, July 3, after the sun went down, it turned foggy. Real thick river fog. And dangerous, too.

But Captain Cannon was *determined* to win, no matter what happened to his passengers. So he ran the *Lee* all night long, through the fog. Right up over the rocks in the Grand Chain and all.

Captain Leathers tried to make a go of it for a while, but he thought it was too dangerous. So he tied up to the bank —like he was supposed to do—and sat it out for close to six hours. Five hours and fifty-five minutes, to be exact. Because it was 12:35 in the morning of July 4 when Captain Tom tied up at Sheppard's Landing, about twenty-five miles above Thebes.

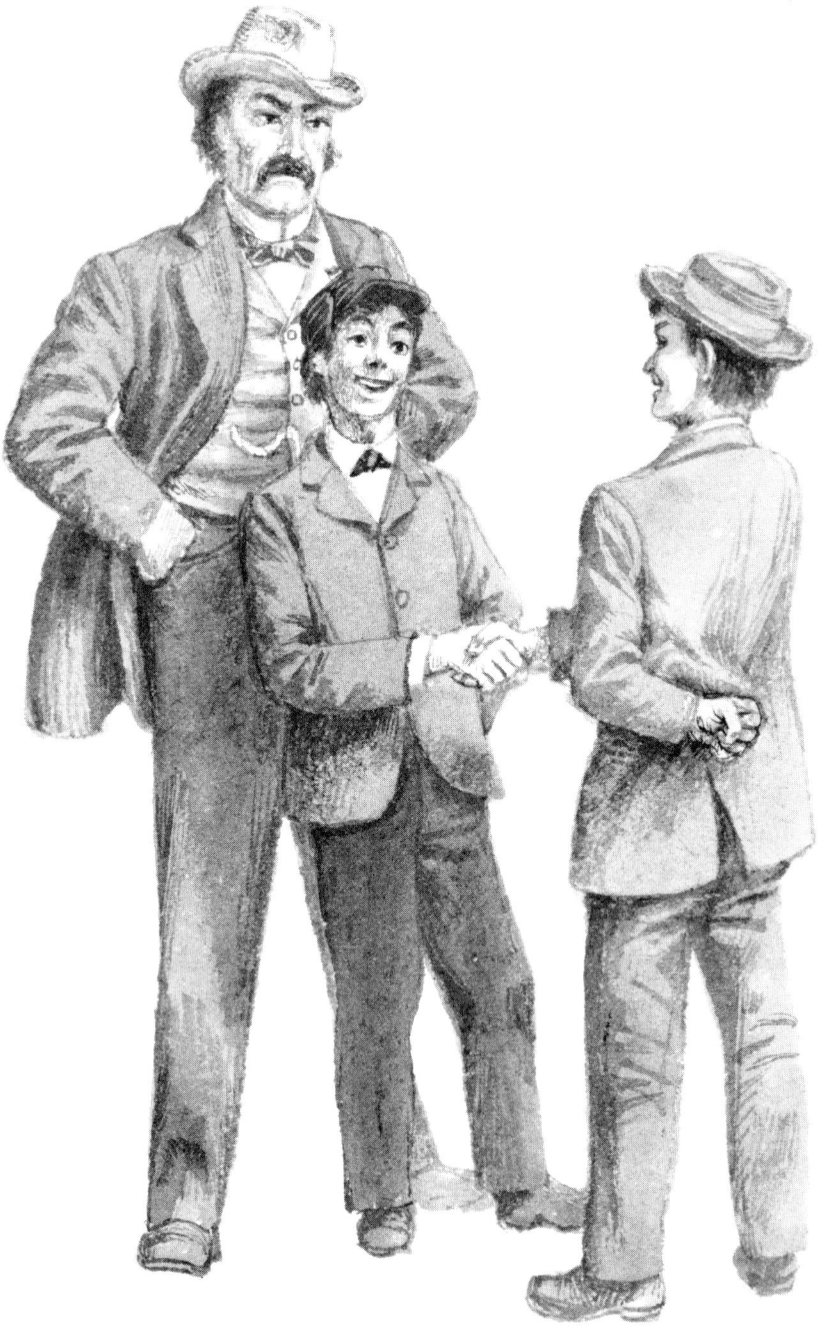

The Bitter End

He said: "The *Natchez* is going to sit here until it's safe to proceed, race or no race."

And he wouldn't budge until the fog had lifted, around 6:30 in the morning. Of course, there wasn't any question of winning the race after that. Pa and me knew we'd lost. And I knew my gold eagle was gone for good.

"Willie," said Pa, "you may have lost ten dollars. But if you don't turn that money over to that Fallon boy with a good firm handshake, and a grin on your face, I'm going to belt the *daylights* out of you. You had no business gambling it in the first place. But since you did it, you're going to learn how to lose. In style!"

I just said, "Yes, sir." I understood what he meant perfectly well.

We heard that the *Robert E. Lee* pulled into the Walnut Street landing in St. Louis well before noon on Monday morning. It was the Fourth of July!

There was huge crowds waiting there, and cannons booming. Robert E. Lee's daughter, Mary Lee, was there to greet Captain Cannon. We heard that after the *Lee* docked, so many people tried to clamber on board, Captain Cannon was afraid they was going to swamp his ship!

Cannon not only won the race—he also set a speed record that stands to this day: three days, eighteen hours, fourteen minutes.

I still think he cheated.

The *Natchez* didn't get to St. Louis until after six o'clock in the evening. There weren't any cannons being shot off for us. And there wasn't any danger of our boat being swamped by crowds. We had that solid, empty feeling you have when you *lose*.

A little later on, I had that feeling a second time, when I had to grin at Dennis Fallon, shake hands with him, and

Willie Jasper's Golden Eagle

give him my gold eagle. It's going to be a long time before I see that much money again.

"Well, you big-time gamblers got to learn how to take the bitter with the sweet," said Pa, putting his arm around my shoulder, as we walked up to the Planter's House. When we got to the desk and started to register, the clerk said: "There's a telegram for you, Mr. Jasper. From Alton, Illinois."

It was from Grandmother Parker. It said:

BABY HELEN BORN 6:00 A.M. MARGARET AND BABY WELL.

LOVE, MOTHER.

"You got a *sister*, Willie Jasper!" said Pa. And I could tell, from the way he hollered, how pleased he was.

The next morning we crossed the river to Illinoistown, on the ferry. I looked at the piers of the railroad bridge that Captain Eads was building. It was going up fast.

When we got to the Illinois shore, we walked over to the railroad depot, and Pa bought us tickets home on the Alton and Junction Branch R.R. The man in the ticket window said we'd be in Alton before ten that morning. And we were.

You see what I mean about railroads? That's the way to travel.

BIBLIOGRAPHY

Andrist, Ralph K., *Steamboats on the Mississippi.* New York: American Heritage Publishing Co., Inc., 1962.

Barkhau, Roy L., *The Great Steamboat Race Between the Natchez and the Rob't. E. Lee.* Privately printed, 1952.

Botkin, B. A., *A Treasury of Southern Folklore.* New York: Crown Publishers, 1949.

Bradshear, Minnie M., and Rodney, Robert M., *The Art, Humor, and Humanity of Mark Twain.* Norman, Oklahoma: University of Oklahoma Press, 1959.

Carmer, Carl, and Sirmay, Dr. Albert, *Songs of the Rivers of America.* New York: Farrar & Rinehart, Inc., 1942.

Carter, Hodding, *Lower Mississippi* (Rivers of America series). New York: Farrar & Rinehart, 1942.

Devol, George H., *Forty Years a Gambler on the Mississippi.* New York: Henry Holt and Co., 1926.

Kane, Harnett T., *Natchez on the Mississippi.* New York: William Morrow & Co., 1947.

———, *Plantation Parade: The Grand Manner in Louisiana.* New York: William Morrow & Co., 1945.

Bibliography

Leish, Kenneth W., ed., *The American Heritage Pictorial History of the Presidents of the United States*. New York: American Heritage Publishing Co., Inc., 1968.

Samuel, Ray, Huber, Leonard V., and Ogden, Warren C., *Tales of the Mississippi*. New York: Hastings House Publishers, 1955.

Smith, Reid, and Owens, John, *The Majesty of Natchez*. Montgomery, Alabama: Paddle Wheel Publications, 1969.

Twain, Mark (Samuel L. Clemens) *Life on the Mississippi*. New York: P. F. Collier & Son, Co., 1917.

Wellman, Manly Wade, *Fastest on the River: The Great Steamboat Race Between the Natchez and the Robert E. Lee*. New York: Henry Holt & Co., 1957.

Wharton, Vernon Lane, *The Negro in Mississippi, 1865–1890*. New York: Harper & Row, 1965.

MAPS

The Mississippi (Alton to the Gulf of Mexico) as Seen from the Hurrican Deck. Pub. by Schönberg & Co., N.Y., 1861; and photographed by the Map Division of the Library of Congress.

Plantation Homes on the Mississippi River from New Orleans to Baton Rouge. New Orleans, Louisiana: C. J. Durel, 1966.

Plantations on the Mississippi River from Natchez to New Orleans—1858. New Orleans, Louisiana: Pelican Publishing Co., Inc., 1967.

ABOUT THIS STORY

Since the subtitle of this story refers to "an eyewitness account," I must make an emphatic disclaimer here: for this is fiction. There was nobody on board the *Natchez* named Willie Jasper, for this is an imaginary recreation of that famous steamboat race.

The facts presented, however, so far as I can ascertain them, are entirely accurate. Steamboats came to the Mississippi in 1811 and were to linger on its godlike expanses for well over a century. But most historians agree that the great race between the *Natchez* and the *Robert E. Lee,* in 1870, marked the apogee of interest in that romantic form of transportation.

Readers may be amused to know that after 1885 (when Grover Cleveland became President—the first Democrat to hold that office since the Civil War) Captain Tom Leathers

About This Story

relented, hauled down the Stars and Bars, and consented to fly the American flag on his steamboats.

It is interesting to reflect that steamboats fascinated us Americans for about half a century (1810–60); and railroads for another half century (1860–1910); with airplanes and automobiles occupying the bulk of our attention from 1910 up until the present.

It suggests that we can expect to be offered further transportation innovations and diversions, rather soon.

F. N. MONJO, an editor of children's books for many years, is the author of more than fifteen books for young readers that deal with noteworthy times and events in history. Several of his books have been ALA Notable Books (including *The Vicksburg Veteran*, *The Drinking Gourd*, and *Poor Richard in France*); all have been highly acclaimed by reviewers and readers alike. Mr. Monjo is vice-president and editorial director of the Department of Books for Boys and Girls at Coward, McCann and Geoghegan, Inc. He and his wife have four children and make their home in New York City.

DOUGLAS GORSLINE has written and illustrated a novel for young people, *Farm Boy*, and a visual history of dress, *What People Wore*. He has illustrated many books for children as well as numerous articles on historical subjects for American Heritage Magazine. Mr. Gorsline, also a highly acclaimed contemporary painter, has exhibited his paintings in America and Europe. He now makes his home in France.

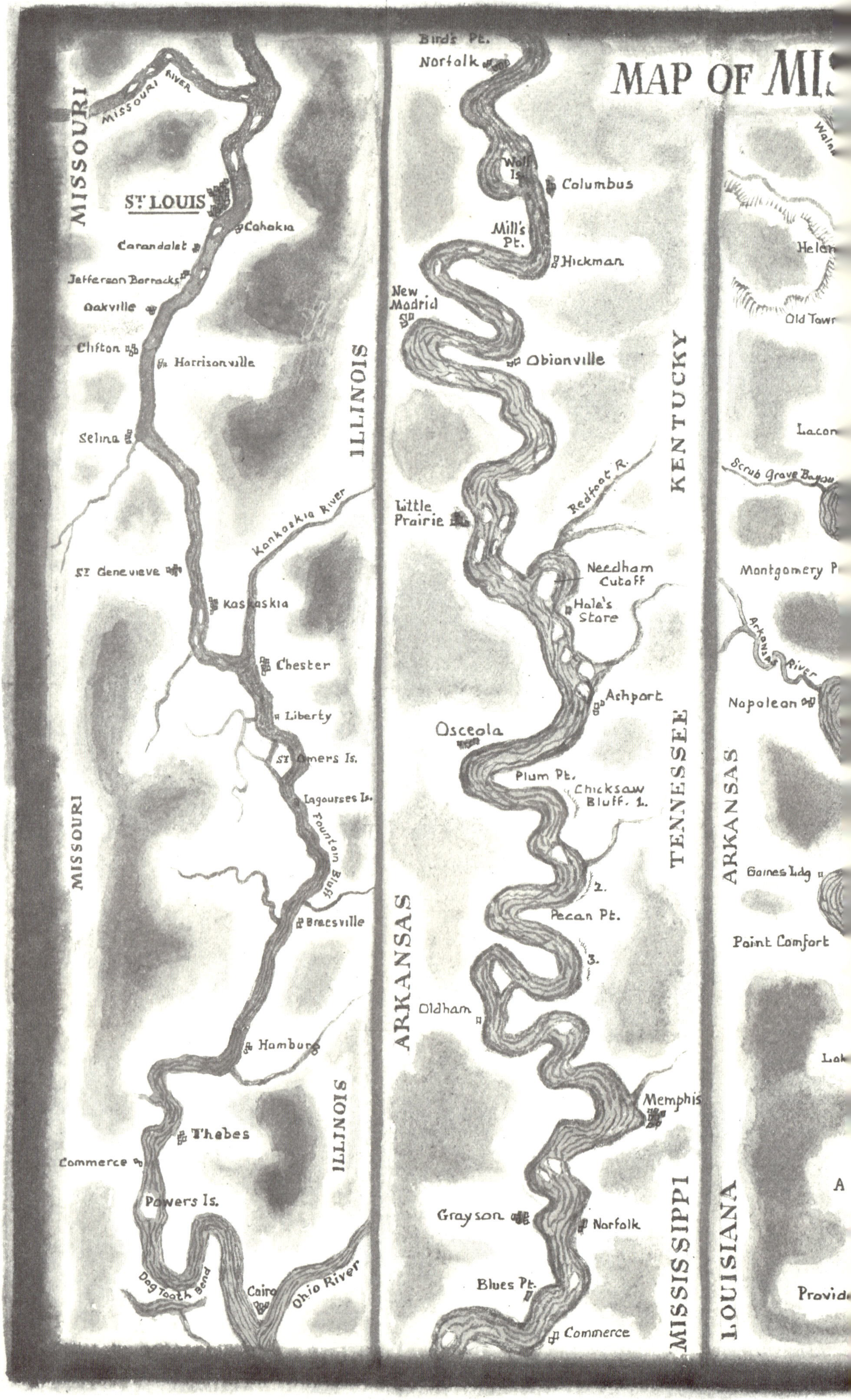
MISSOURI
Missouri River
ST. LOUIS
Cahokia
Carondolet
Jefferson Barracks
Oakville
Clifton
Harrisonville
ILLINOIS
Selina
Kaskaskia River
St. Genevieve
Kaskaskia
Chester
Liberty
St. Omers Is.
Lagourses Is.
Fountain Bluff
MISSOURI
Bracsville
Hamburg
Thebes
ILLINOIS
Commerce
Powers Is.
Dog Tooth Bend
Cairo
Ohio River
Bird's Pt.
Norfolk
Wolf Is.
Columbus
Mill's Pt.
Hickman
New Madrid
Obionville
KENTUCKY
Redfoot R.
Little Prairie
Needham Cutoff
Hale's Store
Ashport
Osceola
TENNESSEE
Plum Pt.
Chicksaw Bluff. 1.
2.
Pecan Pt.
3.
ARKANSAS
Oldham
Memphis
Grayson
Norfolk
MISSISSIPPI
Blues Pt.
Commerce
Scrub Grove Bayou
Arkansas River
Napolean
ARKANSAS
Gaines Ldg
Point Comfort
LOUISIANA